WITHDRAWN

INDIAN THOUGHT AND
ITS DEVELOPMENT

INDIAN THOUGHT AND ITS DEVELOPMENT

BY
ALBERT SCHWEITZER

TRANSLATED BY
Mrs. CHARLES E. B. RUSSELL

THE BEACON PRESS · BOSTON

Copyright 1936 by the Beacon Press
First published in English by Hodder and Stoughton
(London, 1936) and
Henry Holt and Company (New York, 1936)
Beacon Press edition first published in 1952
First Beacon Paperback edition published in 1957
Printed in the United States of America
Second printing, September 1957
Third printing, June 1960

BL
2003
S44
1957x

PREFACE

I HAVE written this short account of Indian Thought and its Development in the hope that it may help people in Europe to become better acquainted than they are at present with the ideas it stands for and the great personalities in whom these ideas are embodied.

To gain an insight into Indian thought, and to analyse it and discuss our differences, must necessarily make European thought clearer and richer.

If we really want to understand the thought of India we must get clear about the problems it has to face and how it deals with them. What we have to do is to set forth and explain the process of development it has passed through from the time of the Vedic hymns down to the present day.

I am fully conscious of the difficulty of describing definite lines of development in a philosophy which possesses in so remarkable a degree the will and the ability not to perceive contrasts as such, and allows ideas of heterogeneous character to subsist side by side and even brings them into connection with each other. But I believe that we, the people of the West, shall only rightly comprehend what Indian thought really is and what is its significance for the thought of all mankind, if we succeed in gaining an insight into its processes.

Like every European who studies Indian philosophy, I am deeply indebted to the scholars who have published the texts and been responsible for the fundamental work of research.

I am specially grateful to Professor Moriz Winternitz of Prague, not only for what I have learnt from his great work on Indian Literature, but also because he has allowed me a share in the wealth of his knowledge by giving me a fund of information in response to my questions.

I have also found it a great advantage to have been able to discuss the problems of Indian thought with my friend Mr C. F. Andrews.

I found Romain Rolland's penetrating studies on Rāmakrishṇa and Vivekānanda very inspiring. And I have to thank my friend Mr A. B. Ashby for valuable help in connection with the English edition.

Indian thought has greatly attracted me since in my youth I first became acquainted with it through reading the works of Arthur Schopenhauer. From the very beginning I was convinced that all thought is really concerned with the great problem of how man can attain to spiritual union with infinite Being. My attention was drawn to Indian thought because it is busied with this problem and because by its nature it is mysticism. What I liked about it also was that Indian ethics are concerned with the behaviour of man to all living beings and not merely with his attitude to his fellow-man and to human society.

But the closer my acquaintance with the documents of Indian thought the more I was assailed by doubts as to whether the view made familiar to us Europeans by the works of Arthur Schopenhauer, Paul Deussen and others—the view namely that

Indian thought is completely governed by the idea of world and life negation—is right. I was compelled to admit the fact that world and life affirmation is present at the back of this thought from the very dawn of its history, and that the existence and interfusion within it of world and life negation and world and life affirmation constitute its special characteristic and determine its development.

I am not merely describing the thought of India, but at the same time I am making a critical examination of it. So far as I can discover, no real discussion of the essential differences between Indian and Western thought has been previously undertaken. Western thinkers either abandon Western thought as did Schopenhauer, Deussen and others, and substitute for it the Indian way of thinking which they have apprehended as pure world and life negation, or with a complete lack of comprehension reject it as if it were something strange and permanently alien.

Nor has any really far-going endeavour been made from the Indian side to understand our thought, which with its immensely varied philosophical systems looks to an Indian like a volcanic landscape.

But there cannot be a total divergence of thought. There are two great fundamental problems common to all thought: (1) the problem of world and life affirmation and world and life negation, and (2) the problem of ethics and the relations between ethics and these two forms of man's spiritual attitude to Being.

Just as I endeavour to understand and gauge Western thought from the standpoint of these two fundamental problems, so now with Indian thought.

Perhaps those who have grown up within the sphere of Indian thought will find it difficult to reconcile themselves to the purely critical nature of my investigation. I ask their pardon in advance. As with Western thought, so now with Indian thought my aim is to examine which ideas are in natural juxtaposition and which are merely, as it were, soldered on to each other. The highest honour one can show to a system of thought is to test it ruthlessly with a view to discovering how much truth it contains, just as steel is assayed to try its strength. My feeling for the profundity of Indian thought and my consciousness of inner relationship to its great representatives both in antiquity and in the present day also find expression in this book.

What may also give offence to Indian readers is my opinion that world and life negation in itself is void of ethics and that the Ahimsa commandment owed its origin not to a feeling of pity, but to the idea of keeping pure from the world, and that it was only later that Ahimsa adopted the motive of compassion. But whatever opinion one may form as to the historical origin of this great ethical principle, it cannot detract from its importance.

The deliberate brevity of my treatise may give occasion to all kinds of misunderstanding. I had no intention of describing Indian philosophy in detail, but only wanted to show how it regards the great problems of life and how it undertakes to solve them. To bring this as clearly as possible into the light of day I drew my sketch with broad, firm lines. This is why anybody who is at home in Indian thought will miss so many details which in his eyes belong to the ideas and thoughts concerned and specially characterise and colour them.

But I believe that such an account as this, which starts from the fundamental problems of thought and is strictly confined to what is essential, is justified.

Everyone who has worked in the same field knows how difficult it is to render into European words the exact meaning of the technical expressions of Indian philosophy. I use these expressions only when it is unavoidably necessary; elsewhere I try to express their meaning in ordinary words.

Technical expressions are a danger for every system of philosophy, whether Indian or European. For they may become formulae which hinder the natural development of thought in the same way as ruts in a road hinder traffic. So to find out what are its real contents it is reasonable to test a system of thought by setting aside the expressions which it has coined for its own use and compelling it to speak in ordinary comprehensible language.

It is deliberately too that I have limited myself to Indian thought and have not also described Indian religious belief, although it is often difficult to define a border-line between the two. I only take religious faith into consideration in so far as it is manifestly governed by the problems of philosophy.

Necessary and interesting as they are in themselves, all arguments from History are of only relative importance where thought is concerned. When Western and Indian philosophy engage in disputation, they must not contend in the spirit that aims at the one proving itself right in opposition to the other. Both are the guardians of valuable treasures of thought. But both must be moving along the path towards a way of thinking which shall pass beyond all the differences of the historical past and eventually be shared in common by all mankind. The real significance of a disputation between Western and Indian thought lies in the fact that each becomes aware of what constitutes the inadequacy of both, and is thereby stimulated to turn in the direction of what is more complete.

For there must indeed arise a philosophy profounder and more living than our own and endowed with greater spiritual and ethical force. In this terrible period through which mankind is passing, from the East and from the West we must all keep a look-out for the coming of this more perfect and more powerful form of thought which will conquer the hearts of individuals and compel whole peoples to acknowledge its sway. It is for this that we must strive.

ALBERT SCHWEITZER

GUNSBACH (ALSACE)
October 1935

CONTENTS

	PAGE
PREFACE	v

CHAPTER I
WESTERN AND INDIAN THOUGHT 1

CHAPTER II
THE RISE OF WORLD AND LIFE NEGATION IN INDIAN
    THOUGHT 19

CHAPTER III
THE TEACHING OF THE UPANISHADS . . . 32

CHAPTER IV
THE SĀMKHYA DOCTRINE 67

CHAPTER V
JAINISM 75

CHAPTER VI
THE BUDDHA AND HIS TEACHING 89

CHAPTER VII
LATER BUDDHISM IN INDIA 121

CHAPTER VIII
BUDDHISM IN CHINA, TIBET AND MONGOLIA . . 138

CHAPTER IX
Buddhism in Japan 150

CHAPTER X
The Later Brahmanic Doctrine 157

CHAPTER XI
Brahmanic World-View in the Laws of Manu . 166

CHAPTER XII
Hinduism and Bhakti Mysticism 174

CHAPTER XIII
The Bhagavad-Gītā 185

CHAPTER XIV
From the Bhagavad-Gītā to Modern Times . 196

CHAPTER XV
Modern Indian Thought 209

CHAPTER XVI
Looking Backward and Forward . . . 250

Index 267

CHAPTER I

WESTERN AND INDIAN THOUGHT

WE know very little about any thought except our own, especially about Indian thought. The reason why it is so difficult to become familiar with this is that Indian thought in its very nature is so entirely different from our own because of the great part which the idea of what is called world and life negation[1] plays in it. Whereas our modern European world-view[1] (Weltanschauung), like that of Zarathustra and the Chinese thinkers, is on principle world and life affirming.[1]

World and life affirmation consists in this: that man regards existence as he experiences it in himself and as it has developed in the world as something of value *per se* and accordingly strives to let it reach perfection in himself, whilst within his own sphere of influence he endeavours to preserve and to further it.

World and life negation[1] on the other hand consists in his regarding existence as he experiences it in himself and as it is developed in the world as something meaningless and sorrowful, and he resolves accordingly (*a*) to bring life to a standstill in himself by

---

[1] The reader must accustom himself to these and similar forms of expression which more accurately represent the original than various words or paraphrases which might be chosen to suit the context. [Translator's note.]

mortifying his will-to-live, and (*b*) to renounce all activity which aims at improvement of the conditions of life in this world.

World and life affirmation unceasingly urges men to serve their fellows, society, the nation, mankind, and indeed all that lives, with their utmost will and in lively hope of realisable progress. World and life negation takes no interest in the world, but regards man's life on earth either merely as a stage-play in which it is his duty to participate, or only as a puzzling pilgrimage through the land of Time to his home in Eternity.

People commonly speak of an optimistic and a pessimistic world-view. But these expressions do not define the distinction in its essential nature. What determines a man's world-view is not whether, according to his disposition, he takes things more or less lightly or whether he has been gifted with or denied the capacity to have confidence; what is decisive is his inner attitude towards Being, his affirmation or negation of life. World-view consists in a determination of the will. The question is not so much what man expects or does not expect from existence, but what use he aims at making of it. Naturally the attitude towards existence determined by the will can be influenced by a more optimistic or more pessimistic disposition just as it may be by favourable or unfavourable events. But it is not simply the result of that. The most profound world and life affirmation is that which has been hard won from an estimate of things unbiassed by illusion and even wrested from misfortune, whilst the most profound world and life negation is that which is developed in theory in despite of a naturally serene disposition and happy outward circumstances.

The battle for world and life affirmation and world and life negation must be constantly fought and won afresh.

World and life affirmation is natural because it corresponds with the instinctive will-to-live which is in us. World and life negation seems to us Europeans an unnatural and incomprehensible thing because it contradicts this instinctive and intuitive force within us.

The fundamental difference of world-view has nothing to do with difference of race. The Indian Aryans show an inclination to world and life negation, the Iranian-Persian and the European Aryans lean to world and life affirmation. This difference of attitude had its origin in events, and these were reflected in thought.

This does not mean that Indian thought is completely governed by world and life negation and ours by world and life affirmation. In the Upanishads there is also a certain element of world and life affirmation and in many writings in Indian literature it even finds quite strong expression. The problem is just this—the relationship to one another of world and life affirmation and world and life negation as they are found side by side in Indian thought, where world and life negation occupies a predominant position.

In European thought too there are periods when world and life negation is found alongside of world and life affirmation. Hellenic thought in later periods began to have misgivings about the world and life affirmation from which it started. Neo-Platonism and Greco-oriental Gnosticism abandoned it in the first centuries of our era. They were no longer concerned with the activity to which man has to devote himself in the world but with his redemption from the world.

This attitude of despair as it confronts life and the Universe becomes apparent in the Greco-Roman thought of the late-classical period because it was obliged to admit that it could not succeed in bringing world and life affirmation and its knowledge of the Universe into harmony with what happens in the Universe. The men of that time were oppressed by the experience of historical events of calamitous import to themselves. Bereaved of hope alike in philosophy and in actual world events, they turned in despair to world and life negation.

And Christianity also brought European thought into relationship with world and life negation. World and life negation is found in the thought of Jesus in so far as He did not assume that the Kingdom of God would be realised in this natural world. He expected that this natural world would very speedily come to an end and be superseded by a supernatural world in which all that is imperfect and evil would be overcome by the power of God.

But this form of world and life negation found in Jesus is different from that of India. Instead of denying the material world because its gaze is directed to pure Being, it only denies the evil, imperfect world in expectation of a good and perfect world which is to come.

It is characteristic of the unique type of the world

and life negation of Jesus that His ethics are not confined within the bounds of that conception. He does not preach the inactive ethic of perfecting the self alone, but active, enthusiastic love of one's neighbour. It is because His ethic contains the principle of activity that it has affinity with world and life affirmation.

In the late-classical period the Greco-oriental and Christian forms of life-negation came together, so that European thought up to the end of the Middle Ages was under the influence of world and life negation. This is clear from the fact that in these centuries the European was so much concerned with the winning of redemption that he took no trouble to move energetically for the improvement of social conditions and the bringing about of a better future for humanity.

But during the period of the Renaissance, and in the centuries which followed, world and life affirmation triumphed. This change was brought about by the influence of the revival of the philosophy of Aristotle and Stoicism, by the faith in progress which owed its rise to the great discoveries of science and by the effect which the ethic of Jesus, with its challenge to active love, had on the minds of men who had been taught by the Reformation to read the Gospels. This form of world and life affirmation was so strong that it no longer took any account of the form of world and life negation which was present in the thought of Jesus. It assumed as a matter of course that Jesus by His preaching had intended to found the Kingdom of God on this earth and that it was man's part to work for its further development. So that, through the principle of activity in His ethics, Christianity, in spite of its original content of world and life negation, was able to join forces with the modern European world and life affirmation.

In the 17th century therefore began the period of the great social reforms on which modern European society is based.

In the latest European thought world and life affirmation has in many respects lost the ethical character which it possessed up to the second half of the 19th century. But this form of world and life affirmation, which has become independent, curiously enough no longer possesses the same strength as that of the earlier period. In the philosophical works of the last decades world and life affirmation is not infrequently expressed in a way that suggests it is wandering on the wrong track and has lost confidence in itself.

Thus both in Indian and in European thought world and life affirmation and world and life negation are found side by side : but in Indian thought the latter is the predominant principle and in European the former.

In the profoundest form of world and life affirmation, in which man lives his life on the loftiest spiritual and ethical plane, he attains to inner freedom from the world and becomes capable of sacrificing his life for some end. This profoundest world and life affirmation can assume the appearance of world and life negation. But that does not make it world and life negation : it remains what it is—the loftiest form of world and life affirmation. He who sacrifices his life to achieve any purpose for an individual or for humanity is practising life affirmation. He is taking an interest in the things of this world and by offering his own life wants to bring about in the world something which he regards as necessary. The sacrifice of life for a purpose is not life negation, but the profoundest form of life affirmation placing itself at the service of world affirmation. World and life negation is only present when man takes no interest whatever in any realisable purpose nor in the improvement of conditions in this world. As soon as he in any way withdraws from this standpoint, whether he admits it to himself or not, he is already under the influence of world and life affirmation.

* * *

The difficulty of the world-view of world and life negation consists in the fact that it is impracticable. It is compelled to make concessions to world and life affirmation.

It really ought to demand of man that, as soon as he reaches the conviction that Non-Being is to be regarded as higher than Being, he shall quit existence by a self-chosen death. It gives a reason for not demanding this of him by explaining that it is not so important to make an end of life as soon as possible as it is to mortify as thoroughly as we can the will-to-live in our hearts. The world-view of world and life negation is therefore in contradiction with itself in that it does want to be lived. With this desire it enters on the path of concession to world and life affirmation which it must then follow to the end.

To remain alive, even in the most miserable fashion, presupposes some activity conducive to the maintenance of life. Even the hermit, who is most strict of all men in his world and life negation, cannot escape from that. He picks berries, goes to the spring, fills his drinking-cup, perhaps even washes himself now and then, and feeds his companions the birds and the deer as a proper hermit should.

Passing from concessions to concessions, which have to be made if men who live the world-view of world and life negation are to remain alive, the decision is reached that what really matters is not so much actual abstention from action as that men should act in a spirit of non-activity and in inner freedom from the world so that action may lose all significance. In order not to be obliged to confess to themselves how much of world and life negation is abandoned, they have recourse to a method of regarding things which savours of relativity.

But the greatest difficulty for the world-view of world and life negation comes from ethics. Ethics demand of man that he should interest himself in the world and in what goes on in it; and, what is more, simply compel him to action. So if world and life negation really becomes concerned with ethics at all, it is driven to make such great concessions to world and life affirmation that it ceases to exist.

To escape this fate it has to try to confine itself to a non-active ethic. This ethic which keeps within the bounds of world and life denial can only demand two things of man, namely that in a spirit of kindliness completely free from hatred he should seek true inner perfection, and that he should show forth this by refraining from destroying or damaging any living thing, and in general by abstaining from all acts not inspired by love and sympathy. Active love it cannot demand of him.

But ethics can only be adapted to this renunciation demanded by world and life negation so long as they have not yet reached their full development. When morality really attains to consciousness of itself, to further the work of love becomes a matter of course which cannot be avoided.

In measure as the world-view of world and life negation becomes ethical, it necessarily therefore renounces itself.

And as a fact the development of Indian thought follows the line of ever greater concessions, until at last, as ethics gradually expand, it is forced either to unconfessed or to admitted abandonment of world and life denial.

But on the circuitous paths which it follows, the thought of India encounters questions and forms of knowledge which we who follow the straight road of our modern world and life affirmation either do not meet at all or do not see so plainly.

We modern Europeans are so much occupied with our activity within the world that we give little or no heed to the question of our spiritual future. But the world-view of world and life negation sets the question of man becoming spiritually more perfect at the centre of all reflection and deliberation. It holds before man as the highest aim that he should endeavour to attain to the right composure, the right inwardness, the right ethical attitude of mind and to true peace of soul. Although the ideal set up by Indian world and life negation of becoming spiritually more and more perfect is of necessity one-sided and inadequate, nevertheless it has great significance for us in affording an insight into a system of thought which is occupied with a great problem of which we take far too little notice.

Our world and life affirmation needs to try conclusions with the world and life negation which is striving after ethics in order that it may arrive at greater clarity and depth.

In ethics, too, Indian thought, starting from world and life negation, presses forward to a stage of knowledge which is quite outside the purview of European thinking. It reaches the point of taking into account the fact that our ethical behaviour must not only concern our human neighbour but all living things. The problem of the boundlessness of the field of ethics and the boundlessness of the claims which ethics make upon us—a problem from which even to-day European thought is trying to escape—has existed for Indian thought for more than two thousand years, although Indian thought too has not yet felt its whole weight nor recognised the whole range which it covers.

* * *

And distinguishing Indian world-view from ours, there is yet another difference, which lies just as deep as that between world and life affirmation and world and life denial. That of India is monistic and mystical, ours is dualistic and doctrinaire.

Mysticism is the perfected form of world-view. In his world-view man endeavours to arrive at a spiritual relationship to the infinite Being to which he belongs as a part of Nature. He studies the Universe to discover whether he can apprehend and become one with the mysterious will which governs it. Only in spiritual unity with infinite Being can he give meaning to his life and find strength to suffer and to act.

And if in the last resort the aim of a world-view is our spiritual unity with infinite Being, then the perfect world-view is of necessity mysticism. It is in mysticism that man realises spiritual union with infinite Being.

Mysticism alone corresponds to the ideal of a world-view. All other world-views are in their nature incomplete, and fail to correspond with the facts. Instead of providing a solution of the fundamental question how man is to become spiritually one with infinite Being and from this solution as a beginning deciding in detail what is to be his attitude to himself and to all things in the Universe, these other forms of world-view lay down precepts about the Universe to instruct man about what part he ought to play in it.

The theory of the Universe which these doctrinaire world-views represent is dualistic. They assume two principles in the history of events starting from the very origins of Being. One principle is conceived as an ethical personality who guarantees that what happens in the Universe has an ethical goal; the other is represented as the natural force dwelling within the Universe and operative in a course of events governed by natural laws. This dualistic world-view exists in very many variations. In the teaching of Zarathustra, in that of the Jewish prophets and in Christianity what happens in the Universe is interpreted as a battle in which the supernatural ethical power wins its way through in conflict with the natural non-ethical. Where a more critical form of thought engages in the problem, it strives in so far as it can to cover up the dualism. But it is there nevertheless. Even the philosophy of Kant is dualistic. It works with the idea, derived from Christianity, of an ethical creator of the Universe without making clear to itself how it can succeed in identifying him with the Primal Cause of Being.

The dualistic world-view does not correspond with reality, for it comprises doctrines about the Universe which cannot be made to square with the facts. It derives from a habit of thought which is under the influence of ethical belief.

So whilst Indian thought rests in the perfected form of world-view, in mysticism, our own thought strives after a form of world-view which is essentially naïve and not in agreement with facts.

How can this be explained?

It is true that mysticism is in its nature the perfected kind of world-view. But if we regard the contents, all mysticism down to the present is unsatisfying, because it denies the world and life and has no ethical content. And the reason for this is that in the history of the Universe and therefore also in the first origins of Being no ethical principle can be discovered.

No ethics can be won from knowledge of the Universe. Nor can ethics be brought into harmony with what we know of the Universe.

For this reason thought finds it impossible to attain to the conception of a spiritual union with infinite Being from which shall emerge the idea of self-devotion to the world in ethical activity. This explains why up to now mysticism really understands by man's becoming spiritually one with infinite Being that he is merely passively absorbed into that Being.

So the remarkable paradox emerges that thinking, when it is in agreement with facts, is unable to justify the world-view of ethical world and life affirmation. If nevertheless it wants to advocate this because natural feeling holds it for true and valuable, it must substitute for real knowledge of the Universe a dualistic ethical explanation. It may no longer regard the Universe as something that has issued and continues to issue from the mysterious Primal Cause of Being, but must assume a Creator of the Universe who has an ethical character and sets an ethical purpose before world events.

According to this ethical explanation of the Universe, man by ethical activity enters the service of the divine world-aim.

As long as thought is still naïve, the ethical-dualistic explanation of the world causes it no difficulty. But in measure as thought develops, so it comes more or less clearly to take account of the unreliability of such an explanation. That is why the dualistic method of thought in European philosophy is not unopposed. A monistic-mystical tendency repeatedly rises in revolt against it. In the Middle Ages, Scholasticism has to be on the defence against a mysticism which goes back to Neo-Platonism and grows strong in independent thinking. The pantheism of Giordano Bruno is a confession of monistic mysticism. Spinoza, Fichte, Schelling and Hegel are concerned with the spiritual union of man with infinite Being. Although their philosophy does not pose as mysticism, it is mysticism nevertheless in its essentials. It is monistic thought under the influence of modern natural science that undertakes the great forward push against dualism.

In actual fact the monistic method of thought, the only method in harmony with reality, has already gained the victory over the dualistic. But it is not able to make full use of what it has won. For it is not in a position to replace the world-affirming ethical world-view of dualism by another world-view of anything like the same value. What monism makes known as its own world-view is altogether beggarly. And what little world-view it has is for the most part borrowed from the world-view of dualism. European monism is not clear as to the necessity of creating a world-view which in its essence is mysticism and which has for its object the question of the spiritual union of man with infinite Being.

The dualistic method of thinking is maintained in Europe because it belongs to the world-view of ethical world and life affirmation, which stands firm because of its inner content of truth and its inner worth. So far as is possible it fits in with monism. The con fusion in modern European thought has its origin in the fact that dualism wears the cloak of monism and monism gets its world-view from dualism.

In India, again, monistic mysticism has to make concessions to dualism in measure as it assumes an ethical and world and life affirming character. It does this in such a way that it passes from the Brahmanic mysticism of being merged in the original source of Being into the Hindu mysticism of loving self-surrender to the one and only God. It arrives, therefore, at a position which it originally avoided, a position where it comprehends the primal source of existence as a divine Being. Here as a matter of fact it abandons monism. But it cannot do otherwise. In order to absorb into itself thoughts of ethical world and life affirmation, and to give correspondingly more satisfaction as a world-view, it is forced to develop into a mysticism of spiritual union with God. In so far then as an ethical nature is attributed to God, ethical world and life affirmation does gain a footing in mysticism.

The ethical conception of God in modern Indian thought is no longer essentially different from that in European thought.

But in spite of these concessions to the dualistic mode of thinking, modern Indian thought holds unswervingly fast to the conviction that world-view is mysticism. It holds to the principle that all the ideas contained in a world-view must together result from the nature of the spiritual union of man with infinite Being. That his world-view is a personal experience of the thought of the individual, in which experience he gets clear about his relationship to Being and, along with this, clear as to what use he wants to make of his life—to this truth the Indian thinkers remain faithful to-day just as they did in the past.

It is true they cannot make a reality of the ideal of which they confess themselves adherents. Their mysticism is inadequate in its nature as in its content. But what a magnificent thing it is that they do not abandon the ideal!

European thought on the contrary has difficulty in

holding fast to the right conception of world-view. In so far indeed as it admits dualism, it completely surrenders this. Dualism regards world-view as a doctrine which the individual has to acquire, instead of its claiming, as does mysticism, to be a conviction which is born, and is constantly being renewed, within him.

But once the true conception of world-view is abandoned, there arises the danger that tenets which are no longer world-view at all nevertheless make their appearance as such. This is happening in the European thought of our own time. Opinions and convictions which have arisen from no kind of reflection about man and the Universe, but which are only concerned with man and human society, are given out as world-view and accepted as such, in the same way as we are content to call the history of the miserable wars waged on our little earth Universal History. Nothing is so characteristic of the want of thought of our time as that we have lost the consciousness of what world-view really is.

It is necessary that we come back to the understanding that the only true world-view is that which arises from meditation in which man is alone with the Universe and himself.

If such confusion and perplexity reign in European thought, it is not only due to the difficulties which it has to overcome, but to the fact that it is not sufficiently clear about its real task, the task namely of creating a world-view. European thought only finds its right bearings when all the single problems which affect human existence converge into the fundamental problem of how man can arrive at the right spiritual relationship to Being. It only raises its head when it again sets the highest goal before it.

*   *   *

There is, then, a twofold interest for European thought in the study of the thought of India which is so different in its nature, let alone the stimulus of becoming acquainted with a foreign mode of thinking.

In the first place, European thought represents a world and life affirmation which is wanting in depth because it has not yet come to a thorough understanding of its position in relation to world and life negation and to ethics. In Indian thought, after a long struggle against world and life negation, ethical world and life affirmation prevails. The problem with which we are concerned is here unfolded like a scroll from the opposite end.

And secondly, European thought allows itself to be guided by the knowledge that the world-view of ethical world and life affirmation is, from its content, the most valuable, whilst Indian thought is determined by the other fact, that mysticism is the perfect kind of world-view. European thought, then, has to make an effort to attain to a world-view of ethical world and life affirmation which in its nature is mysticism, and Indian thought has to strive to give to mysticism ethical world and life affirmation as its content. Again, then, the problem with which our thinking is concerned is unrolled in Indian thought from the opposite end.

In Indian thought we learn to understand better what is going on in our own thought.

From a comparison of European and Indian thought it becomes clear that the great problem of thought in general consists in the attainment of a mysticism of ethical world and life affirmation. Thought has not yet succeeded in uniting into a single whole the world-view which in its method is perfect and the world-view which is most valuable in content. It cannot master the puzzling difficulties which are in the way of this apparently so simple synthesis. But it must not on that account cease to aim at that world-view which alone is really satisfying. Up to now it has directed its efforts far too little towards this end.

* *

*

CHAPTER II

THE RISE OF WORLD AND LIFE NEGATION IN INDIAN THOUGHT

HOW does the thought of India arrive at world and life negation?

When Hellenic thought turns towards world and life negation, it is because in the end it begins to have misgivings about the world and life affirmation which for centuries had seemed a matter of course. It cannot bring this into harmony with knowledge of the world and the tragic events of History. It surrenders itself to world and life denial, because it loses its original energy and reaches a point where it despairs of the Universe.

In the thought of India, on the other hand, world and life negation does not originate in a similar experience. It is there from the very beginning, self-originated, born as it were in a cloudless sky. And it is there in a very curious guise. Unlike Hellenic world and life negation, it does not claim to be generally accepted, but remains on good terms with world and life affirmation, which it allows to exist alongside of it.

As we can see in the hymns of the Veda, the Aryans of Indian antiquity still passed their lives in a state of quite simple joy in existence. In these hymns, which were sung in accompaniment to the act of sacrifice. the singers of that epoch supplicate the gods to bestow on those who provide the sacrificial gifts great herds of cattle and horses, success in all their undertakings, wealth, victory in battle and long life. Further, they express the expectation that they themselves will be well rewarded by the god whose praise they happen to be singing. " If I, oh Indra, were like thee the only lord of wealth, then would he who sang my praise be the owner of cows ", is the utterance of one among them.

Aryans (Sanskrit *ārya* ; ancient Persian *arıya*), that is to say lords, is what the members of the Indo-Iranian peoples in Hindustan, Persia and Eastern Iran called themselves.

As we know now from the results of archaeological research in the region watered by the Indus, the Aryans who migrated into India found there a civilisation which was already considerably developed and bore an unmistakable resemblance to the civilisations of Sumeria, Elam and Mesopotamia. It is impossible to determine to what race the carriers of this civilisation belonged, whether they were immigrants from south-west Asia or natives of the country who were possibly identical with the pre-Aryan Dravidian population. For these Dravidians, whose language was quite different from that of the Indo-Aryans, already possessed a considerable civilisation. Among the Dravidian languages are Tamil, Telugu, Malayalam and Canarese, which are now spoken in Southern India.

We do not know exactly when the migration of the Aryans through Afghanistan into India began, but it may well be reckoned as earlier than 1500 B.C. First of all the invaders conquered the Panjāb, that is to say the land of the five rivers that come from the Himalayas and join the Indus, and the territory of the Indus itself, that is to say, therefore, the whole of North-west India. Later they penetrated to the south-east, to the plains of the Ganges and the Jumna. They certainly reached Southern India before the year 300 B.C. Here, however, they were unable to supplant the Dravidian civilisation and religion in the same way as in the north.

The Veda (Veda means knowledge) consists of several parts (Samhitas), the first of which, the Rig-Veda (Song Veda), is in ten books, containing 1028 hymns. The most venerable of these hymns may well go back to earlier than 1500 B.C.; the latest date from about the 10th century B.C. Agni, the god of fire and light, Indra and Varuna are the gods most celebrated in song.

The other parts of the Veda—the Sāma-Veda, the Yajur-Veda and the Atharva-Veda—at least in their present form are later than the Rig-Veda. For one can see in them that the Aryan conquerors have meanwhile reached the country of the Ganges. The hymns of the Rig-Veda only refer to the Panjāb.

The Sāma-Veda consists of only 585 single stanzas. These correspond to the melodies in use at the sacrifice. As no musical notation was yet known, the best-known stanza-text belonging to the melody to which it is scored is indicated.

The Yajur-Veda contains the liturgies and prayers from which a selection can be made for the various acts of sacrifice. (Sacrifice for New and Full Moon, Sacrifice for the shades of the departed, fire Sacrifice, Sacrifices for the seasons, Soma Sacrifice and animal Sacrifice.)

The Atharva-Veda is so called after the oldest priests, the Atharvans, whose concern was the worship of fire. These corresponded to the fire-priests (Āthravans) of the religion of Zarathustra. Formulae for charms and incantations in the form of songs, of which many certainly go back to remote antiquity, form the contents of the Atharva-Veda.

But even as early as in the hymns of the Rig-Veda we can already see the thought from which world and life negation developed. In these hymns we encounter men who know they are uplifted above this world. They are the Shamans and medicine-men—later called Yogins—who get themselves into a state of ecstasy through drinking the intoxicating Soma, through mortification of the flesh and by self-hypnosis. Thus possessed, they regard themselves as beings into whom the gods have entered, and believe themselves in possession of supernatural powers.

This consciousness of being uplifted above the world which is experienced in ecstasy is the condition determining Indian world and life negation. We do not know in how far these Shamans and medicine-men of olden days really carried world and life negation into effect in their lives. But it is quite certain that they never thought of demanding it of other people. They regarded this state of being uplifted above the world as something that only came under consideration for themselves because they possessed the capacity of attaining to community with the gods.

The word Yogin is connected with a root which is present in the Latin *jungo* (I join) and the German *Joch* (yoke). By concentrating on themselves and the supra-earthly, the Yogins attained to the power of falling into ecstasy and experiencing union with the Divine.

The Soma beverage was prepared with much ceremony from the juice of a plant. " We drank Soma, we became immortal, we found the gods ", so runs a hymn of the Rig-Veda about Soma-drinking.

Among the Brahmins the idea of being exalted above this world had already resulted in an attitude of world and life negation. But what is characteristic is that they did not carry out world and life negation consistently, but at the same time made room beside it for a certain element of world and life affirmation. They passed the first part of their lives in world and life affirmation. They had house and farm, founded a family and were anxious to increase their property. In return for the sacrifices which they offered, they demanded plenteous gifts in the form of cattle. If a king organised a Brahmin debate, he must have ready a prize of hundreds of cattle for him who triumphed over the others in erudition. The generous King Janaka, whose life lay between about 800 and 600 B.C., even went so far as to tie a gold coin to the horns of each of the thousand cows destined for the victor. This same Janaka asks the great Brahmin Yājñavalkya when he appears before him whether his desire is for profound discussion or for cows. " For both, great King ", is his reply.

Thus the Brahmin lives for his family and his possessions until his sons in their turn have established households. But then he resigns himself to world and life negation and withdraws from the world. He devotes his life to asceticism, mortification of the flesh, meditation and exercises in self-submergence, that is to say to the concentration on himself and the Supra-sensuous which leads to ecstasy. Sometimes he chooses death through hunger, fire or water.

Originally magicians (Shamans) and priests were probably identical. But with the development of sacrificial worship, and its demands for special qualifications, there arose a special order of priests.

The Brahmins could not pass their whole lives in world and life negation because they were priests. They had to concern themselves with the maintenance of the family in which were inherited the knowledge and the secrets requisite for the efficacious offering of the sacrifice.

So long as they were officiating as priests, they were in union with the Spiritual through the word of sacrifice (Brahman), that is to say through the ancient formulae sung and recited when the sacrifice was offered. Later, in their old age, they experienced union with the Spiritual by means of exercises in self-submergence, and thus attained the power of leaving the world as beings who resembled the gods.

World and life negation in ancient Indian thought had, then, no connection with a world-view. It had nothing to do with man as such, but was only for the super-men who as magicians or priests had the right to enter into communion with the supra-sensuous Might and thus to attain to supernatural power. They alone had anything to gain by world and life negation. It was their privilege. It was of no use to ordinary people.

So Indian world and life negation was originally associated with a magical idea dating from prehistoric times. It developed through the experience of withdrawal from the world in a state of ecstasy.

An attempt has been made to understand world and life negation as something that the Aryan conquerors had adopted from the aboriginal inhabitants they found in India, along with magic-religious ideas such as were now found in the Atharva Veda. According to this view, world and life negation and magic-religious ideas were originally foreign to Aryan Thought. The fact that in Brahmanic Thought alongside world and life negation we find also life and world affirmation would, then, have to be traced back to the other fact that at periods subsequent to the first conquest there arrived in India fresh migrations of

Aryans. These new immigrants would have endeavoured once more to make the world and life affirmation current among them accepted in opposition to the world and life negation which the first conquerors had taken over from the aborigines. Thus among the Indian Aryans themselves there would have been a struggle between world and life affirmation and world and life negation, and in this way it might be claimed that in the Upanishads world and life negation and world and life affirmation are both represented.

This hypothesis cannot be supported. We know nothing of the thought of the aboriginal inhabitants. The view that the Aryan conquerors took over from them both world and life negation and magic-religious concepts can in no way be proved. And moreover, it was not the Aryan immigrants as such who adopted world and life negation, but only the Brahmins.

Just as little can it be proved that the magic-religious ideas of the Veda originated with the aboriginal population. The fact that in the Avesta there are similar conceptions makes it probable that we are here concerned with views which were common to the primeval Aryans when they still formed a single people.

And further there is nothing in the Upanishads which allows us to infer that there was any conflict between world and life negation and world and life affirmation. They simply stand there side by side.

The simplest hypothesis is then that the Aryans were originally all followers of world and life affirmation, and that world and life negation originated among the Brahmins under the influence of the idea of being exalted above this world which was developed from magic-religious ideas and the experience of ecstasy. Only in this way is it comprehensible that the idea of world and life denial in the more ancient period was only represented by the Brahmins, or, to put it better, by certain circles among the Brahmins, whilst the people held fast to the world and life affirmation which was natural to them. World and life negation belonged to a sacerdotal form of thought which was developed alongside popular thought.

Not Brahmins alone, but, as we gather from various evidence, members also of the warrior caste had a share in originating the world of thought we find in the Upanishads. We do not know in how far they made effective the idea of being exalted above the world of the senses to which their thought attained in world and life negation.

* * *

But who are the Brahmins?

In the hymns of the Rig-Veda they have not begun to play any part. It is only in the Atharva-Veda, and therefore when the Aryans have already reached the Ganges country, that we meet them as the highest representatives of the priesthood.

At the same period too comes the development of the caste system, to which there is no reference in the older Vedic hymns.

Four main castes are distinguished: (1) The Brahmins; (2) the Kṣatriyas (warriors); (3) the Vaiśyas (craftsmen and agriculturists); (4) the Śūdras (menials). Beside these there are also mixed castes (outcasts). Lowest of all are the Cāṇḍālas, who on the mother's side are descended from Brahmins and on the father's from Śūdras. Pariah is the name given to outcasts in Southern India. The members of the three first castes are Aryans, those of the others are descendants of the aboriginal population.

The Brahmins regard themselves as super-men. They are convinced that even the gods are subject to the supra-sensuous Power to which they themselves are united. The sacrificial act is for them not so much an offering to the gods with thanksgiving and supplication as a magical transaction by which they make the denizens of heaven serviceable to themselves through the medium of the supra-sensuous Power which is over them as well. And this, in their belief, takes place through the sacrificial utterance named Brahman. The ancient word Brahman is approximately equivalent to " sacred power ". The members of the priestly caste are called Brahmins (Brāhmaṇas) as being men who are united to this Power.

The idea that power is exercised through magic formulae is found also in the hymns of the Rig-Veda. According to the Vedic conception the gods govern the world through spells and magic melodies. In one of the hymns we find the phrase, " Singing, some (gods) devised the great melody by which they made the sun shine forth ". The curious thing about the Brahmins is that they claim for themselves power which is of the same nature as that of the gods. They believe, for example, that the sun would not rise if they failed to celebrate the sacrifice of fire in the early morning. They regard themselves as " human gods ".

To understand the thought which arose among them, one must realise this enormous self-consciousness of the ancient Brahmins. The Indian Aryans as such might just as well have arrived at a world-view of ethical world and life affirmation as the Persian Aryans. The religion of the Vedic hymns is of a world and life affirming nature and contains ethical elements. Agni, Varuna and Mitra meet us in this religion as ethical divinities. Varuna is the guardian of the sacred law, to whom people confess their sins in order to ask of him forgiveness. And in the Vedic hymns also monotheistic tendencies assert themselves. The highest divinities are no longer kept severely separate, but even at this early period form a composite personality with various names.

But the Brahmins failed to further the evolution from polytheism to ethical monotheism which was here in preparation and for this reason it did not reach its natural conclusion. No prophet-priest like Zarathustra arose among them to transform and complete the traditional religion in conformity with the demands of ethics. The Brahmins showed no interest in the higher development of the religion of the people. They were not preoccupied with ethics. Not religion but their priesthood and their sacerdotal power was the object of their thought. Their whole endeavour was directed to piercing deeper into the secret of the Supra-sensuous to which they drew near as priests by means of the incantations accompanying the act of sacrifice, and with which they became one in the state of ecstasy.

Now this magical mysticism nevertheless contained the possibility of developing into a mystical world-view. Although only in a primitive fashion, it was indeed concerned with the question of becoming one with infinite Being. So it was like a bud from which a world-view could unfold. For this to happen all that was necessary was that for the Brahmins the Supra-sensuous should become a non-magical instead of a magical value. And this in fact is what happened.

At the outset the Brahmins were still fast prisoners of the belief that the secret of the Supra-sensuous lay hidden in the sacrificial rites, in the words of sacrifice, and in the myths on which these were based, and that it might be discovered there. So with this in view they undertook to investigate and interpret the four divisions of the Veda, in which work the most arbitrary etymologies and allegories play the principal part. This was the beginning of Brahmanic thought which is so hard for us to understand.

But then gradually they began further to concern themselves with the problem of the Supra-sensuous by natural observation and reflection. The secrets of nature gained significance in their eyes alongside those of sacred tradition. Among these their attention was attracted by the connection between life and breath, by sleep, dreams, the facts that the plant is contained in the seed and salt in sea water. To be able to explain these and other enigmas of daily life, they assumed that all corporeal existence contains a non-corporeal, and that a spiritual world underlies the world of the senses. From being a force exercising control over existence by magic, the Transcendental became for them something which belongs to existence in the ordinary course of Nature. So the doctrine was developed that the real essence of all things is something immaterial and eternal which derives from the primal cause of the Immaterial, from the World-Soul, and that it participates in the World-Soul and returns to it.

The Supra-sensuous in its entirety, the All-Soul (World-Soul), they called the Brahman. They used therefore the same expression for it as they used for the words of sacrifice. Thus it becomes clear that what they were originally concerned with was acquiring knowledge of the magical Primeval Force to which they addressed themselves in the potent sacrificial incantation. The word Brahman is derived from the root b.-r̩.-h., to be strong.

Under the influence of popular imagination the impersonal Brahman develops into a Brahman-divinity. This Brahman-divinity is represented as the highest God. It is the God Brahman for instance, who according to later tradition appears to the Buddha and determines him not to keep the knowledge of redemption for himself alone, but to communicate it to the world.

Probably the conception of the Brahman-divinity arose under the influence of the Hindu cult of Vishn̩u-Siva. The Brahman-divinity is the Hindu supreme God under the name given by the Brahmins.

Next we find the expression Ātman coming into use to denote the Supra-sensuous. The root of this word is probably the same as that of the German word *atmen* (to breathe), in which case it means breath.[1] And as, for the Brahmins, the breath is the expression of the non-corporeal in man, they first use the word Ātman for the immaterial part of the individual. Later they advance to the use of the same word for what is immaterial in the whole universe. Their designation of the Brahman also as " Ātman " shows us the transformation taking place in their thought.

But to become one with pure Being is something quite different from union with the magic Primeval

[1] But nothing can be said with absolute certainty about the etymology of the word Ātman (or Tman) which is found as early as in the Rig-Veda.

Force which was originally the object of priestly thinking. Now it is no longer a question of a union with the Supra-sensuous possible only for Brahmins and Yogins, but of a union which concerns man as man, and a union which has significance for the conduct of his life. From magical mysticism a mystical world-view has evolved.

The Brahmanic world-view is focussed on world and life negation, because it goes back to the magical mysticism of union with the Supra-sensuous by withdrawal from the world.

* *
*

CHAPTER III

THE TEACHING OF THE UPANISHADS

THE prelude to Brahmanic thought is sung by some of the later Vedic hymns, in which is raised the question of the highest Divine Principle which lies behind all the gods and the relation of this Principle to the Universe. The theme is developed in the Brāhmaṇas and the Upanishads.

These prose texts dating from somewhere between 1000 and 550 B.C. contain meditations on the secret meaning of the sacrificial rites and words, and of the myths, and along with these sections large and small in which untrammelled reflection is devoted to the investigation of the Supra-sensuous.

In the Brāhmanas, which date from earlier than the Upanishads, the new thought is still quite in its beginnings.

The Brāhmaṇas and Upanishads therefore fall far short of offering a coherent presentation of the Brahmanic doctrine of Universal-Soul-in-All-Things. This is only found in them in fragments, some large, some small. And in addition these fragments are the work of various schools and various ages. Those who have described the Upanishads as chaotic are not altogether wrong.

The older texts are called Brāhmaṇas because they treat of knowledge about the Brahman (the sacrificial incantation).

The word Upanishad is derived from a verb " to sit down beside somebody ". It means " confidential communication ". The Upanishads accordingly contain the secret instruction about the real teaching of the Veda (by which is meant the doctrine of becoming one with the Supra-sensuous) imparted to the Brahmin pupil by his teacher.

There is an old saying that the relation of the Upanishads to the Veda is that they are the life-sap of life-sap and ambrosia of ambrosia.

The four parts of the Veda, the Brāhmaṇas and the Upanishads are regarded as sacred revelation. For centuries they were handed down only by word of mouth.

As is well known, the Indo-Aryan characters are derived from an old Semitic alphabet which we have learnt from Phoenician inscriptions and from the characters engraved on the famous stone of the Moabite king, Mesa (about 890 B.C.). We do not know when writing came into use among the Indian Aryans. They probably learnt the art from Phoenician traders. The most ancient witness to Indian writing is given by the edicts chiselled partly on rocks and partly on pillars of stone in which the celebrated Buddhist king, Asoka (272–231 B.C.), exhorts his subjects to a moral and religious way of life. He commands them to display " a well-meaning demeanour towards slaves and servants, deference to persons worthy of honour, gentleness to living creatures, generosity to Brahmins and ascetics ".

But even long after writing had come into use, the Vedas, Brāhmaṇas and Upanishads were only handed down orally. For they contain knowledge which was meant solely for Brahmins and must not get among the people. Not a sentence of them must be uttered before members of the lower castes. It was only many centuries after Christ (the exact date cannot be traced) that they were first written down.

What an achievement of the memory to know these long texts by heart! What a number of years (in the Upanishads there is talk of twelve) the Brahmin pupil had to pass with his teacher before he had made them his own! During the time he was occupied with memorising and meditating, he tended the teacher's cows and served the sacrificial fires.

The language of these sacred texts is Sanskrit, an ancient Indian language closely related to ancient Persian. It was probably still a living language in the first centuries of our era. To-day it plays in India the part that Latin played in mediaeval Europe. Sanskrit means the aristocratic language of culture in contrast with the common, uncultured tongue, Prākrit.

The world of thought of the Upanishads first became known in Europe through the Oupnek'hat. The Oupnek'hat (the word came into being by a mutilation of Upanishad) is a selection of sixty sections of the Upanishads translated into Persian by Prince Mohammed Dara Shakoh in the year 1656. A Frenchman, Anquetil Duperron (1723–1805), brought this work to Paris with the Avesta and 180 other MSS. he had collected in India, and published it in two volumes (1801–1802) with the addition of a Latin translation by himself.

In the 18th century the principal study in Europe had been Chinese thought in so far as it had become known through translations of the works of Confucius (Kung-Tse) and Meng-Tse (Mencius) by missionaries working in China. From the beginning of the 19th century interest turned to Indian philosophy, of which something began to be known through the first Indian scholars in England (Warren Hastings, Charles Wilkins, William Jones, Thomas Colebrooke, Alexander Hamilton) and through the publication of the Oupnek'hat. In the year 1808 Frederick Schlegel, who had enjoyed the teaching of Hamilton in Paris from 1803–1804, published his book *Concerning the Language and Wisdom of the Indians*, which made a great stir.

Arthur Schopenhauer drew his knowledge of Indian thinking almost exclusively from the Oupnek'hat.

The French orientalist Eugène Burnouf (middle of the

19th century) rendered great service in the first investigation of the Vedic texts.

* * *

The Brahmins, then, taught as a great secret the mysticism of the identity of the souls of all beings and all things with the Universal Soul. According to this mysticism all that is of the nature of soul belongs to the Universal Soul. Man carries the Universal Soul within him. And because the Universal Soul dwells in all Being, it finds its own self again in all Being, in the life of plants as in the life of gods. This is the meaning of the famous *Tat twam asi* (That thou art thyself) of the Upanishads.

The Doctrine of the Universal One and the Universal Presence of Soul in the words of the Upanishads:
" That verily from which these beings originate, by which, having originated they live, to which, departing, they return again—endeavour to understand that ! that is the Brahman." [1]—" The Soul of created beings is a unity, only divided between creature and creature ; unity and plurality at the same time, like the moon mirrored in many waters." [2]—" The Brahman serves as a dwelling for all living things and dwells in all living things." [3]—" This is the truth : as from a bright fire come thousands of sparks like itself, so from the Unchanging come all kinds of living beings and return to it again." [4]—" Who sees himself in all beings and in himself all beings sees, enters into the highest Brahman without any other reason." [5]—" The highest Brahman, the Soul of all, the great mainstay of the universe, more subtle than the subtle, the eternal Being, that art thou, that thou art " (*Tat twam asi*).[6]

[1] Taittirīya Upanishad, iii. 1.   [2] Brahmabindu Upanishad, xii.
[3] Brahmabindu Upanishad, xxii.   [4] Mundaka Upanishad, ii. 1.
[5] Kaivalya Upanishad.   [6] Kaivalya Upanishad, vi.

In deep sleep, according to the Brahmins, the soul temporarily abandons its connection with the body in order to unite itself completely with the Brahman. In dreams it proves its freedom from the body by moving in a world of the senses which is quite other than that in which it lives when it is united with it.

The Brahmins therefore conceive sleep, that unfathomable secret, as a transitory state of death.

The Brahmanic mysticism of identity with the Infinite is then of quite a different nature from European mysticism. In the latter man gives himself up to the Infinite in humble devotion and in the Infinite is absorbed; in Brahmanic mysticism he realises with pride that in his own being he carries infinite Being within himself.

Compared with the Brahmanic super-man, Nietzsche's is a miserable creature. The Brahmanic super-man is exalted above the whole universe, Nietzsche's merely over human society.

The result of the freedom of the soul from the world of sense, as preached by Brahmanic mysticism, is that man has to pass his life completely detached from all that is earthly. His thoughts must be entirely directed to the world of pure Being. Just as a man carried away from his own country with his eyes bandaged when released in a strange land has to ask his way to his home from village to village and rests not till he reaches it; thus it is, according to a metaphor used in the Upanishads, that man must conduct himself in this world.

" When all desires which live in his heart disappear, then man becomes immortal. Here already he reaches the

Brahman. As the old slough of a snake lies on an ant-hill, so now does the body lie there." [1]

Even in one of the Brāhmanas there is a saying to the effect that the heavenly world cannot be reached by him who offers sacrifice to the gods but only by him who sacrifices himself.

On the basis, then, of the Brahmanic doctrine of union with pure Being, world and life negation develops into a demand for a world-view. It ceases to have significance for Brahmins and Yogins alone. The original view that only Brahmins and Yogins can be united to the Brahman is now replaced by the other view that to the Brahman every human soul belongs. From this time on world and life negation is valid for man as man.

So in the Upanishads we find a whole series of sayings in which complete renunciation of the world is recommended and praised as the only sensible attitude. As we know from the Brhad-Āraṇyaka Upanishad, the great Brahmanic teacher Yājñavalkya was one of the representatives of this view. The true Brahmins, in his eyes, were those who desired neither sons nor property, but were only concerned with the Eternal and had therefore given up everything and gone forth into the world as beggars. That was the life he chose for himself. Before starting on his wanderings he divided his property between his two wives, Maitreyī and Kātāyani, and on this occasion Maitreyī begged him to give her some instruction about the Eternal because such knowledge is the only valuable possession.

But to become one with the Brahman not only

[1] Bṛhad-Āraṇyaka Upanishad, iv. 7.

demands renunciation of the world, but in addition the concentration of the spirit on the Supra-sensuous. Detailed instructions on how to practise this concentration are given in the Upanishads. The repetition of the sacred sound "Om" plays a great part in such exercises in self-submergence. What is aimed at in this Yoga practice is ecstasy, the psychical experience of union with pure Being.[1]

One must never forget that the Brahmanic doctrine is not to be understood as if union with the Brahman can result from reflection by the light of reason. Many passages of the Upanishads indeed give this impression. But the real belief of the Brahmins is that man does not attain to union with the Brahman by means of any achievement of his natural power of gaining knowledge, but solely by quitting the world of the senses in a state of ecstasy and thus learning the reality of pure Being.

The Brahmanic doctrine is concerned with a truth that must not merely be known, but also experienced.

*   *   *

Although we find in the Upanishads a series of passages in which, by reason of the doctrine of union with the Brahman, complete renunciation of the world is demanded, the Brahmin community as such, as I have already pointed out, does not conform to

[1] The expression "Yogin" is first found in the later Upanishads. In the Rig-Veda (x. 136) the man in the state of ecstasy is called Keśin (the long-haired). The oldest word for ascetic is Muni. It is often found in the Rig-Veda. Ancient expressions for ascetics are "Sannyāsin" (he who renounces), "Śramana" (he who takes great pains) and "Parivrājaka" (the wanderer).

this ideal of life, but leaves to world and life affirmation its rights beside world and life negation. Brahmanism has the courage to be inconsistent and not draw the full conclusions from the knowledge to which it has attained.

It manages to combine world and life affirmation and world and life negation in such a way that it allows the Brahmin to pass the first half of his life in world and life affirmation and only the second half in world and life negation.[1]

We possess only very insufficient information about the struggle which took place in the Brahmanism of the period of the Upanishads between world and life affirmation and world and life negation, or about the development of the priestly ideal of life which sought to reconcile contradictions. In the most ancient Upanishads there is no completely developed doctrine of the various stages of life (Āśramas). This was first set forth in a passage of the Jābāla Upanishad.[2]

Four Āśramas are here distinguished : schooldays with a teacher ; life as father of a household ; life of retirement in the forest ; the life of solitary wandering when the world is completely renounced.

According to the Kaṭhaśruti Upanishad, after the Brahmin has given up the sacrificial service, he shall "start on his long journey" either through hunger, fire or water, or he shall begin the ascetic life as a wanderer.[3]

---

[1] See also pp. 22, 23.
[2] Jābāla Upanishad, 4. According to Professor Winternitz the word *Āśrama* is derived from the root *śram*, and originally meant the religious efforts of ascetics and forest hermits. It came to be used to describe a hermitage as a place for religious endeavour.
[3] Kaṭhaśruti Upanishad, ii. 3.

What prevented the Brahmins from giving full approval to the radical world and life negation really demanded by the Upanishad doctrine of the Brahman and union with the Brahman was their conviction of the necessity of their priestly calling and the carrying on of their priestly race. So they arrived at regarding the duty imposed on them by their caste as an obligation that must be fulfilled before world and life negation could enter on its rights.

They were also withheld from complete renunciation of the world by the demands made on them by the cult of the manes of the departed. They could not resolve to be unfaithful to their duties to the spirits of their ancestors and they could not renounce the begetting of descendants who would offer sacrifice to their own manes. So hallowed traditions would not permit them to put into practice the complete world and life negation which resulted from their knowledge of the Brahman. Some of them night decide the struggle in favour of entire renunciation of the world, but the caste, as such, could not do so. It had to find a means of compromise to secure the continuance of the sacrifices to the gods and the due performance of the rites of the manes.

The custom among the Brahmins of relinquishing their priestly calling at the approach of old age, and in expectation of death manifesting their exaltation above the world and their relationship to the Brahman by renunciation of the world, had existed possibly since remote antiquity. For the practice of passing the closing period of life in world renunciation can also be explained by the old magic mysticism of becoming one with the Brahman, and not only by the mysticism of the Upanishads. In this case the priestly ideal of life, in which world and life negation replaces world and life affirmation, would not have first originated in the struggle between world and life affirmation and world and life negation which was going on in the period of the Upanishads, but would have been already given in established tradition. If this assumption be correct, the Brahmins are protected by the current tradition of the priestly ideal of life from drawing the logical conclusions from the doctrine of union with the Brahman and from upholding the demand for the radical renunciation of life as that doctrine is developed in the Upanishads.

We must notice that the Brahmins only set up an ideal of life for themselves. The question how men in the other castes—women were not considered in this connection—were to decide in the matter of world and life affirmation and world and life negation was not really attacked at all as early as the Upanishads, although they represent a mysticism in which union with the Brahman is no longer possible for the Brahmin alone, but attainable by man as such.

Perhaps the famous saying of Yājñavalkya about the true Brahmin[1] is to be understood in the sense that even those who are not members of the caste of Brahmins can become Brahmins in spirit by striving after knowledge of the Eternal and renouncing the world. In the Upanishads there does not seem to be any anticipation of the fact that large numbers of members of other castes devote themselves to world and life negation because of the doctrine of the Brahman and union with the Brahman.

In general, it is clear that no great movement for the realisation of world renunciation resulted from the Brahmanic mysticism of union with the Brahman, although it contained the idea of world and life nega-

[1] See p. 37.

tion. It was only with Jainism and Buddhism that world and life negation began its great offensive. But this offensive did not start from the mysticism of union with the Brahman, but from the doctrine of reincarnation. It was only when the idea of reincarnation began to interest the masses, and when fear of constantly returning to existence began to rule men's minds, that there arose the great movement towards renunciation of the world which then continued for centuries. Deliverance from reincarnation can only be attained through freedom from the world and freedom from the will to live.

In the doctrine of reincarnation, world and life negation became a much more efficacious force than it was in the Brahmanic mysticism of union with the Brahman. It was strengthened there by the idea of redemption. In the Brahmanic mysticism the important point is not so much redemption from the misery of existence and liberation from the world as the experience of being exalted above the world in union with the Brahman.

Because Brahmanism had set up for itself an ideal of life containing world and life negation and world and life affirmation side by side, it became a dam which stemmed the flood-waters of world and life negation which burst forth in Jainism and Buddhism. It is of fundamental importance for the history of the spiritual life of India that the Brahmins on principle maintained the rights of marriage and the family against all onslaughts of radical world and life negation.

*   *

*

Brahmanic mysticism has nothing to do with ethics. It is through and through supra-ethical.

The Brahmins have the courage to admit to themselves that nothing ethical results from meditation on the Universe. They attribute no ethical qualities to the supra-sensuous Primal Cause of the Universe. This allows them to remain entirely in the monistic habit of thought. But it compels them also to understand becoming one with infinite Being as a pure act of the spirit which has nothing to do with ethics.

To be exalted above the world means for the Brahmins : to be above all action, good as well as evil. They frankly express this.

In one Upanishad it runs : " The immortal man overcomes both the thoughts—' I did evil ' and ' I did good '. Good and bad, done or not done, cause him no pain." [1]

The Brahmins of the period of the Upanishads make no attempt to give ethical meaning to world or life denial and the mysticism of union with the Brahman. Easy as it would be to turn the doctrine of *Tat twam asi* in an ethical direction, they nevertheless neglect to do it. That man has to see himself in all beings and all beings in himself, they only take as meaning that he must presume in them the same world-soul which he carries in his own breast. They do not demand that by reason of this relationship with them he shall have sympathy for them and show pity towards them. The great command not to kill and not to injure living creatures plays no part as early as the Upanishads, although it is already mentioned in them—but in very few passages.[2]

[1] Brhad-Āranyaka Upanishad, iv. 4.
[2] Two of these passages are found in the Chāndogya Upanishad

If the Brahmins of certain circles speak out against animal sacrifice, they do so only because they regard it as unnecessary, not because they are opposed to such slaughter.

But observe: the Brahmins do not assert that it is all the same whether man does good or evil. Their teaching of " Beyond good and evil " is quite other than that of the Gnostics and Nietzsche. They know only a non-activity which is exalted above good and evil, but not a similar activity. The right to take no account of good and evil is only possessed, according to them, by the man who for the sake of union with the Brahman devotes himself to renunciation of the world and to inactivity. Such a one is released from the duty of doing good. And further, his evil deeds are henceforth as little taken into consideration as his good ones. He attains to union with the Brahman simply and solely by knowledge, renunciation of the world and self-submergence.

On the contrary, whoever remains in ordinary life must keep to the customary conceptions of good and evil valid in general for what should be done or left undone. So we find in the Upanishads beside utterances which establish the supra-ethical character of the doctrine of identity with the Brahman others which uphold the rights of traditional ethics. Naturally they specially deal with commands and prohibitions valid for Brahmins and Brahmanic pupils who are still in ordinary life.

The Brahmin is commanded to speak the truth, to fulfil his caste-duties, to study the Vedas, to be careful

(iii. 17 and viii. 15). In the second of these, killing is forbidden in general " except on a sacred spot ", that is to say, in the sacrifice.

that the thread of his race is not broken off, to watch over his possessions, to honour the gods, the shades of his ancestors, his parents and his guest, and to control his desires. For the unmarried Brahmin pupil the strictest abstinence is made a duty. Theft, drunkenness, adultery with the wife of his Brahmin teacher and murder of a Brahmin are named as specially criminal acts.

Love and pity for one's fellows are still beyond the horizon of these ethics. Great importance on the other hand is laid on truthfulness.

All over the world the evolution of ethics is such that its first great achievement is the high estimation of truthfulness. Man makes the forward step from lower to higher ethics, not by the recognition of any kind of obligation of kindness to his neighbour, but by his condemnation of lying, deceit and perfidy.

The duty of truthfulness always occupies the first place with the Brahmins.

In one of the Upanishads a youth comes to a Brahmin to seek acceptance as a pupil. In answer to the question whether he is really of Brahmin descent, he confesses that he is the son of a maid-servant, born in her youth when she wandered much in the world. She had not been able to tell him who his father was. " Only a Brahmin can speak so frankly ", says the teacher, and accepts him as a pupil.

The Brahmins do not merely teach truthfulness: they observe it as well. When their thinking leads to the recognition of facts which will endanger their privileges and interests, they do not draw back. They, who regard it as the privilege of their birth and station to be in relationship with the Suprasensuous, get so far as to preach the doctrine that man as such is called to this estate. They, whose office it is to offer the sacrifices, and who draw their income from this source, depreciate the value of sacrifice and declare that the one thing needful is right conduct and perfect knowledge.

The Brahmins therefore may be credited with this great and exceedingly rare achievement that as priests they are altogether intent on truth! Truthfulness blooms as a marvellous flower in the glacier landscape of their chilly world-view. Inadequate as is their morality, it has an essentially distinguished quality.

Reverence for truth comprises for the Brahmins reverence also for law as such.

In the Bṛhad-Āraṇyaka Upanishad, which is one of the oldest, there occurs the passage: " Law is dominion over dominion. Therefore there is nothing higher than law. Through the law the weaker masters the stronger as through the King. The law is equal to the truth." [1]

Beside the command to truthfulness the Brahmins place the command to fulfil the duties of caste. Action in conformity with caste is regarded as something grounded in the divine order of the Universe. It is sacred and sets certain bounds to world and life negation. In obedience to the obligations of caste, the Brahmins remain in ordinary life and the priestly office until they begin to grow old, although they know from their youth up that union with the Brahman will be only attained in renunciation of the world and inactivity.[2]

---

[1] Bṛhad-Āraṇyaka Upanishad, i. 4, 14.
[2] See in addition p. 40.

Whilst the Brahmins except from action in general the practice of the activity prescribed by caste, and attribute to this in some measure a necessity required by the order of the Universe, they recognise that the world and life negation demanded by their mysticism of union with the Brahman cannot be maintained and carried out without a great concession to world and life affirmation.

* * *

In the Upanishads we find also the doctrine of reincarnation (Saṃsāra), which is also called the doctrine of the transmigration of souls (Metempsychosis).

In what relationship does this stand to the Brahmanic mysticism of identity with the Universal Soul? Does it belong to it intrinsically or is it something separate that establishes itself beside it? The latter is the case.

The hymns of the Rig-Veda knew nothing as yet of a cycle of re-births. In that ancient period people hoped for their departed ones that they entered into the heavenly world of the gods. And for this they relied less on their good works than on rightly performed and numerically adequate sacrifices and magic rites. There is no mention, save in hints, of the fate of those who did not attain to this state of bliss.

In the Brāhmaṇas there is something about those who have entered into blessedness suffering a second death in the Beyond after some time has elapsed. But how we are to imagine this " second death ", and whether from this idea is derived that of re-birth on earth, remains obscure.

The doctrine of reincarnation belongs originally to a myth which describes the wandering of the departed to the realm of bliss. It explains the waxing and waning of the moon by its absorbing the souls that come from the earth and after a certain time sending them on to heaven, or down again to the earth in rain. The doctrine of reincarnation appears in the Upanishads in connection with this myth.

" All who depart from this world go to the moon. The waxing half fills itself with their lives ; in the waning half it is effecting their re-birth. The moon is the gate of heaven. He who knows how to reply to it, him it allows to pass by. He who cannot reply, him it sends, changing itself into rain, down to the earth in rain ; he is re-born here and there according to his deeds and knowledge as worm, moth, fish, bird, lion, wild-boar, jackal (?), tiger, man or whatever it may be. For when a man comes to the moon, the moon asks : Who art thou ? Then he ought to answer : I am thou. . . . If he speaks thus, then the moon lets him get away out above itself." [1]

Of course the myth originally said that the moon gives free access to heaven to those who have accomplished the requisite good works and sacrifices. That it only does so when a soul knows how to answer it glibly with the doctrine of *Tat twam asi* belongs to the form given to the myth by the Brahmins in order to incorporate it with their doctrine of union with the Brahman through the highest knowledge.

According to the original myth further, it is not all the dead who arrive at the moon but only those who are destined for eternal bliss or for re-birth into human existence. We learn this from two Upanishads.[2] Men who are to become

---

[1] Kauṣītaki Upanishad, i. The Bṛhad-Āraṇyaka Upanishad, vi. 2, and the Chāndogya Upanishad, v. 10, also refer to the visit of souls to the moon.

[2] Bṛhad-Āraṇyaka Upanishad, vi. 2, and Chāndogya Upanishad, v. 10.

animals experience this change straightway after their death, or—the texts are not clear about this—after a visit to a place of punishment. The moon is originally thought of only as a place of joy.

* *
*

The doctrine of reincarnation has something Brahmanic about it in so far as it assumes that the souls of men, animals and plants are of like nature.

Attempts have been made to show that the moon myth from which the doctrine of reincarnation derives was not of Aryan origin, but originally belonged to the religious imaginary world of the aboriginal inhabitants of India and was then adopted by the Aryans. This view cannot be supported by evidence. But it might be adduced in its favour that in the Vedic hymns there is no trace of the moon myth concerning reincarnation, whilst it is quite alien to the mysticism of union with the Brahman.

Although the doctrine of reincarnation has in common with the Brahmanic teaching the conception of the like nature of all souls, nevertheless—a point which is usually overlooked—it is not yet in agreement with the Brahmanic mysticism of the identity of individual souls with the Universal Soul. The relationship of individual souls to the state of being in the body and to the Universal Soul is quite different in the doctrine of reincarnation from what it is in Brahmanic mysticism.

According to the teaching of the Brahmins, all individual souls after their existence in the world of the senses are without further ado reabsorbed into the Universal Soul. Every cessation of bodily existence is equivalent to a final return of the soul concerned into the Universal Soul, just as every beginning of bodily existence is conceived as a new manifestation of soul in the world of the senses. The Brahmins assume, then, that there is a continuous influx of soul-stuff into the material world and a continuous return-flow out of it. The metaphor used in the Upanishads of the fire from which new sparks are constantly mounting into the air and falling back into it again is characteristic of their views.

According, then, to the Brahmanic teaching, every soul in the corporeal world is new to it, visits it but once and automatically participates in re-union with the Universal Soul without any knowledge or achievement on its own part being required of it. The souls of wild animals and plants return into the Universal Soul in the same fashion as that of the Brahmin who possesses the profoundest knowledge and has advanced furthest in asceticism and self-submergence. For it is not as if the Brahmin only gains union with the Universal Soul through knowledge, asceticism and submergence of the self. All he gains through these things is the advantage that he knows about the blessed state that awaits him and already enjoys it in this world, inasmuch as he passes his life on earth in inner and outer freedom from the material world and in meditation directed entirely to the Universal Soul.

It is true there are texts of the Upanishads which read as if union with the Universal Soul and the immortality which accompanies it were only attained through knowledge, asceticism and renunciation of the world. But the real meaning of the doctrine is not laid open to question by such inexact statements.

Brahmanic mysticism is concerned with the idea

of being exalted above the world, not with the idea of redemption. The doctrine of reincarnation, on the other hand, starts from the premiss that souls are prisoners in the world of the senses. The question of how they can return into the Universal Soul becomes therefore the real problem. They must earn their redemption. The Brahmins teach that souls are automatically and naturally free from the world and, in so far as they are capable of such knowledge, only need to recognise and experience their freedom.

To acquiesce in the doctrine of reincarnation means, therefore, for the Brahmins the giving up of their own belief about the relationship of the individual soul to the material world and the Universal Soul in favour of a different view, and involves allowing the freedom of the soul from the material world, which for them presents no problem, to become a problem.

And further. If the Brahmins adopt the idea of redemption contained in the doctrine of reincarnation, they create for themselves difficulties they cannot master. According to their own teaching they must assume, not only for the human soul, but for all souls in the bodily state, a return into the Universal Soul. The question of world-redemption is for them posed and solved.

But if they agree to the doctrine of reincarnation, they can neither state the question nor solve it. The doctrine of re-birth is really concerned only with the redemption of mankind. It makes liberation from the corporeal dependent on knowledge and conduct of which only human beings of the highest development are capable. So world-redemption can only be imagined as that all souls in the material world, rising from one form of existence to another by degrees, enter into the highest human existence and in this win the capacity of return into the Universal Soul. It is of course impossible seriously to think of making the sea of soul-stuff contained in the material world thus flow back into the ocean of Universal Soul as it were through the pipe of a village pump.

If Brahmanism acquiesces in the doctrine of reincarnation, it can no longer really hold fast to the idea of universal redemption which necessarily belongs to its mysticism of Soul-in-All-Things.

The Gnostic systems of the late Hellenic period are concerned with the redemption of the totality of soul-stuff held prisoner in the material world. What is going on in the Universe becomes for them the great drama of the entrance of soul into matter and its resultant return from it at the end of the ages.

Such a historical method of contemplation—the only method which can be directed towards the problem of world-redemption—lies far from Indian thought. It is, moreover, based on the hypothesis of the appearance of a personal redeemer. This hypothesis is first found in India in the post-Buddha period. Later Buddhism (Mahāyāna-Buddhism) makes a personal redeemer of the Buddha. Starting from the standpoint of the historical method of regarding things which has been thus arrived at, it occupies itself once more with the question of world-redemption, which for centuries had lain on one side in the thought of India.

Not even the redemption of mankind is able to make the doctrine of reincarnation satisfactorily comprehensible. As a punishment for their evil courses, it makes men enter into the existence of despised and savage beasts. But how they can work their way up again from this to a higher existence—this question remains unsolved. The doctrine of reincarnation at this point contradicts itself. It must make the attainment of the higher mode of existence dependent on ethical behaviour. But how can the soul which has once sunk down into the life of an animal become ethically deserving?

As a matter of fact, the doctrine of reincarnation must regard the redemption of souls which have entered into animal life as practically impossible. This is the conclusion of the Buddha.

* * *

The doctrine of reincarnation rests, then, on quite other premisses than the Brahmanic doctrine of Soul-in-all-Things, and suffers from serious deficiencies. It cannot fit in with Brahmanic mysticism.

But how is it, then, that the Brahmins came to adopt it?

To begin with, it is in itself so important and is held in so great esteem that they cannot ignore it. And secondly, it goes so far to meet them as to assert that the souls of all living things are of like nature. But what is decisive is that it stands in close and living relationship to ethics.

For in face of ethics the Brahmins find themselves in a difficult situation. Their mysticism is supra-ethical. They cannot abandon their principle that union with the Universal Soul is only experienced in knowledge, world-renunciation and self-submergence. But what meaning, then, is left for ethics? It will not do to deny all value to morality. And now the doctrine of reincarnation steps in to give ethics their rights by the side of supra-ethical mysticism and at the same time place this doctrine at the service of ethics.

Ethics gain the important recognition that from ethical or non-ethical conduct there ensues the higher or lower form of re-birth, and that by the constant practice of goodness is finally attained the highest form of existence, in which man becomes capable of the experience of union with the Universal Soul.

According to the original popular doctrine of reincarnation, man attains to the state of heavenly bliss by means of sufficient good works. If they do not suffice, he will be born again as a human being. If the evil that he has committed preponderates, his return is into the existence of an animal. In the process of transformation which this doctrine underwent among the Brahmins, the importance of the ethical element was limited to the proviso that through good works there could never be earned the state of bliss, but only a better reincarnation.

But the doctrine of reincarnation permitted the Brahmins not only to preserve the supra-ethical character of their mysticism and at the same time the prestige of ethics, but in addition made it possible for them to acquiesce on a satisfactory theoretical basis in the fact that the majority of human beings still passed their lives in world and life affirmation. This they explained among themselves by saying that these had not yet participated in the final reincarnation which qualifies men for the knowledge of the true way of redemption. On the ground of the doctrine of reincarnation they could assume also that members of the lower castes will in time arrive at rebirth in the higher and so become capable of redemption.

Thus the doctrine of reincarnation allowed the Brahmins to develop a relativistic method of thought. As the highest, most esoteric truth they could preach a world and life negation exalted above good and evil, and by its side allow the validity of a lower, exoteric truth which leaves ethics and world and life affirmation in possession of their rights.

But Brahmanism paid a heavy price for the advantages it received from the doctrine of reincarnation. It is true that it made them of service to itself. But at the same time it absorbed along with the doctrine a foreign element, and through it became something other than it by nature was. In the period of the Upanishads Brahmanic thought was occupied solely with the question of experiencing union with the Universal Soul. Later on this problem was joined by the question of redemption from the cycle of re-birth which towered above and overshadowed it. For centuries Indian thought was governed by the fear of remaining in the cycle of reincarnation, of which the original Brahmanic teaching knew nothing.

*   *
  *

The teaching of the Upanishads, therefore, is not a homogeneous, self-contained system, but lacks unity and completeness. It comprises a series of problems which give the thought of the following centuries plenty of occupation. Some of these belong to the

Brahmanic doctrine as such; others go back to the difficulties met in reconciling the Brahmanic teaching with the doctrine of reincarnation; others again result from the challenge offered by world and life affirmation and ethics to world and life negation.

* * *

First Problem.—What is really to be understood by the Brahman?

Brahmanic mysticism, like all other, has to do with the question, whether the highest, pure Being, to which man feels in his true self that he belongs, is to be thought of as an impersonal Absolute without attributes, or in some way as the highest spiritual entity. But this question is neither raised nor decided in the Upanishads.

The real opinion of the Brahmins of the period of the Upanishads is to the effect that the Brahman is to be imagined as the impersonal Absolute without attributes. The only thing one can assert of it, according to a saying of Yājñavalkya in the ancient Bṛhad-Āraṇyaka Upanishad, is "Neti, neti" (Not, not). All one knows of it is that it has nothing of empiric being about it.

In the work of Śaṃkara, the great scholastic of Brahmanism (9th century A.D.), is found the story of the instruction about the Brahman which the wise man Bāhva gave to one who was eager for knowledge. When the latter questioned him he was silent. When he had repeated his question a second and a third time, he at last said to him: "Why, I am teaching thee, only thou understandest not: this Ātman is silent"

Beside passages in the Upanishads which treat of the Brahman as the Absolute without attributes, are others far more simply expressed which speak of it as the highest spiritual Being that unites all forms of perfection in itself.

Occasionally also it is represented as the Primal Force which dwells within all Being and maintains all Being. For the Brahmins have begun to be preoccupied with the secret of the life that is in nature. They explain the coming into life of the plant from the seed by the hypothesis that the real essence of the plant is in the seed as a soul that gives shape to it. But in their contemplation of nature they do not get beyond the beginnings. And therefore their doctrine of Soul-in-all-Things is much less living than that of the Renaissance, although here and there it reminds us of that. The conception of force is not yet fully formed among them, and this impedes the development of the doctrine of Soul-in-all-Things.

There are also in the Upanishads passages in which the Universal Soul is conceived as the highest divine Person. One of these runs: " The only God is hidden in all living things, permeates all things and lives as soul in all beings ".

Thus even in the period of the Upanishads there are schools of Brahmin thought which find nothing out of the way in attributing personality to the Universal Soul.

Saṃkara, the Brahmin scholastic of the 9th century A.D., explains these vacillations in the conception of the Brahman by assuming that in the Upanishads there are two different doctrines. One, he says, represents the esoteric truth about the Brahman in that it understands it as the impersonal, unknowable Absolute without attributes; the other preaches the exoteric truth and allows those who are not capable of the highest knowledge to venerate the Brahman as the one and only God, who manifests himself in various divinities.

Of course the Brahmins of the period of the Upanishads did not think of distinguishing between an esoteric and an exoteric doctrine of the Brahman. They preached but one doctrine. It was nothing to them that it lacked unity.

And on the other hand monotheistic Hinduism declares that the Upanishads conceived the Brahman everywhere as a personal God, and that the passages which can be adduced in support of non-personality must be interpreted so as to correspond with the others.

The profoundest thinkers of the Upanishads forgo applying the conception of God which originates in religious tradition to the Primal Cause of Being. But later Indian thought, like European philosophy, is no longer occupied with the question whether and in how far this is possible. It regards *Deus sive Natura* as a matter of course.

* * *

Second Problem.—In what relationship does the Universal Soul stand to the world of the senses? Why does pure Being make its appearance in a material world, and what measure of reality does that world possess?

In quite general terms the belief found in the

Upanishads is that the Universal Soul is enveloped in the material world as it were by a veil. But it has no need of it. On the contrary it is like something foreign around it. The world of the senses has no meaning. The individual soul has to use all its force to free itself from the delusion of thinking it has something to do in it or anything to hope from it.

The more ancient Upanishads accept the world of the senses as something which is real and a matter of course.

But in proportion as Brahmanic thought takes seriously its fundamental knowledge that all that is has proceeded from the Universal Soul, so it must arrive at apprehending the world of the senses as only a manifestation of the Universal Soul. Once on this path it cannot do otherwise than follow it to the end and regard the material world as mere appearance. And in the later Upanishads this in fact is what it does. In these the principle that the Universal Soul is the only reality and that there can be no other beside it is consistently adhered to. This is called the doctrine of non-duality (Advaita).

Now there remains no alternative but to assume that the world of the senses is a magic play (Māyā; māyin means magician) staged by the Universal Soul for itself. The individual soul is brought into this magic play under a spell. By reflection about itself it must become capable of seeing through the deception. Thereupon it gives up taking part in the play. It waits quietly and enjoys its identity with the Universal Soul until, at death, the magic play for it ceases to be.

The Brahmins, therefore, are not contented merely

to establish the fact that the Universe is inexplicable. They undertake to give an interpretation of it which corresponds with world and life negation. And so they arrive at asserting not only its meaninglessness but in addition its unreality.

This explanation of the world fits in admirably with their supra-ethical mysticism of identity with the Universal Soul. But ethics will not fit in with it. The ethic of action above all is hard hit by the assertion that the world has no meaning. Man cannot engage in ethical activity in a world with no meaning. His ethical life in such a world must be limited to keeping himself pure from it.

But if further the reality of the world is denied, then ethics altogether cease to have any importance. The only thing that remains for man to do is to see through the delusion of believing in a material world.

The doctrine of Māyā results logically from the theoretical premisses of the Brahmanic belief about Being. The Brahmins cannot escape it. But by confessing it, they admit they are not in a position to justify even the little they demand in the matter of ethics.

* *
*

Third Problem.—How do individual souls come into existence from the Universal Soul and how are they reabsorbed into it ? The Brahmins of the more ancient period will have nothing further to do with this question. They make shift with metaphors and compare individual souls with the glowing sparks which rise from a fire and fall back into it and with reflections caused by the moon on water.

Now the Brahmanic mysticism could well leave unexplained the issue of individual souls from the Universal Soul and their reabsorption into it. But the doctrine of reincarnation cannot do that. It attributes to the individual soul a far more pronounced individuality than does Brahmanic mysticism. According to it the soul goes through experiences in the world. It has to bear the consequences of the deeds done by men in the world of the senses. But according to pure Brahmanic doctrine it adopts the attitude of a mere spectator in the material world and remains untouched by it.

The doctrine of reincarnation in no way requires the assumption that individual souls have issued from the Universal Soul and will return to it again. Indeed it can do nothing with it. For this doctrine the most natural thing is simply to start from the fact that in a way which cannot be further explained all through eternity there has been an endless number of eternal individual souls (which constitute the spiritual element in the Universe) for which is prescribed the passing of a constantly renewed existence in the world of the senses until finally they succeed in winning liberation from it.

And what need is there to regard liberation from the cycle of re-birth and the return of the soul into the Universal Soul as equivalents ? The doctrine of reincarnation has no interest whatever in asserting such an inexplicable thing as that the individual soul in the end loses its individuality. It is sufficient for it to establish the fact that as a result of the freedom attained the soul is in a state of perpetual bliss.

Strange as it at first appears, thought that really

agrees to the doctrine of reincarnation is therefore involved in difficulty if it holds to the Brahmanic conception of individual souls deriving from the Universal Soul and returning to it again.

* * *

Fourth Problem.—What is the nature of the connection between the individual soul and its bodily manifestation?

In accordance with the genuine Brahmanic teaching, the soul is untouched by the bodily form which for a time belongs to it, whether or no any kind of reality may be ascribed to this, or whether it be held only for an illusion. But the validity of ethics is brought into question by this hypothesis, and that is why the doctrine of reincarnation cannot accept it. If moral conduct is to play any part in the liberation of the soul from the cycle of re-births, the soul must in some way participate in the corporeal and be affected by human experiences and actions.

So the doctrine of reincarnation can in no sense agree to the assertion that the Universe is not real, but must hold fast to its reality. And further—and this is where the real difficulty begins—it has to make comprehensible how soul and body, if we assume that by their nature they have nothing in common, can stand in any relationship to each other whatever. The doctrine of reincarnation has to do with the same question with which later on in Europe the philosophy based on the definitions of Descartes is busied. For this the problem is to explain how it is that in living creatures the body can receive stimuli from the soul and transform these into reality. The doctrine of reincarnation must show how the destiny of the soul is influenced by the action of the body.

* * *

Fifth Problem.—The only significance the Brahmins grant to ethics is that the nature of the reincarnation is determined by good or evil deeds. These then are only a preparation for liberation from the cycle of re-births which can only be attained through highest knowledge, renunciation of the world and self-submergence.

Can morality really be satisfied with this limitation of its importance decreed by the Brahmins in contradiction to religious tradition and natural feeling? Must it not demand a greater part to play in a system of thought which is keenly concerned with the question of deliverance from reincarnation?

* * *

Sixth Problem.—The Brahmins make to world and life affirmation the great concession that they regard the fulfilment of the obligations of occupation dictated by caste as action of a higher order which within certain bounds maintains its rights in face of world and life denial. For themselves they bring the two so into harmony that they work as priests for the first half of their lives and pass the second half in world renunciation.

But now world and life negation have ceased to be only the concern of Brahmins and Yogins. There arose in the period of the Upanishads a real worldview of world and life negation, and consequently the members of the castes of warriors, agriculturists and traders no less than the Brahmins are faced with the challenge to strive for the experience of union with the Brahman, or deliverance from reincarnation, in highest knowledge, world-renunciation and self-submergence. They obey it by devoting themselves in crowds to the monastic life. But what rights do they now concede, alongside world and life denial, to action dedicated to the fulfilment of caste obligations?

Really some sort of settlement ought to have been arrived at to allow the warriors, agriculturists and traders to pass the first part of their lives at their calling, and the latter end in renunciation of the world. But this does not take place. The non-Brahmins assume the right to lead a life of world-renunciation from youth up.[1] But the idea that the fulfilment of the duties involved in membership of a caste has the importance of action of a higher order which may enter into competition with world and life negation is maintained. And then there comes a day when it has made such progress that not only are rights conceded to action of a higher order for a portion of the duration of human life, but such action is placed on an equality with world and life negation and even exalted above it. This happens in the courageous mode of thought which finds expression in the Bhagavad-Gītā.

*   *
*

[1] This occurred also among the Brahmins.

If one would understand what happened in the centuries which followed the period of the Upanishads, one must realise these problems that are found in their teaching. When one first makes acquaintance with Indian thought, with what perplexity one faces the appearance alongside the Brahmanic doctrine of the Sāṃkhya doctrine, Jainism and Buddhism! Trivialities apart, they stand for the same world and life negation as does Brahmanism. Like that they urge man by exercises in self-submergence to endeavour to participate in the experience of detachment from the world in a state of ecstasy. But what right of existence have these systems beside Brahmanism? How can they arise and subsist beside it?

The explanation of the riddle is that these new teachings did indeed allow the façade of world and life denial to stand, but undertook complete rebuilding behind it. They no longer based world and life negation on the idea of the identity of the individual soul and the Universal Soul, but on that of liberation from the cycle of re-births.

The Sāṃkhya system, Jainism and Buddhism accepted the conclusion which follows from the theoretical incompatibility of the doctrine of reincarnation and Brahmanic mysticism. They renounced the latter. The sole task they set themselves was to understand the why and the how of the cycle of re-births and to expound why and how world and life negation can bring it to an end.

But this non-mystical mode of thought, which was busy only with the question of deliverance from reincarnation, could only for a time maintain itself in opposition to mystical thought. Later it gradually lost ground again. The mysticism of identity with the Primal Origin of Being was victorious because it was magnificently simple, carried in itself the profoundest truth and—what was of great importance—was contained in the sacred scriptures which were constantly gaining in repute. This explains how it is that in the course of time the Sāmkhya doctrine was absorbed by Brahmanism, Jainism lost the great importance which it had and Buddhism even ceased to exist in India.

And in the course of this development of Indian thought which stretches over centuries one further phenomenon emerges—that ethics attain to ever greater authority and world and life affirmation wrings ever greater concessions from world and life negation.

* *
*

CHAPTER IV

THE SĀMKHYA DOCTRINE

THE Sāṃkhya doctrine undertakes to investigate the relation of the soul to the world of the senses in such a way that its imprisonment within that world and liberation from it will become comprehensible.

Sāṃkhya means enumeration. The doctrine gets its name from the fact that numbers play a great part in it. Thus, for example, it makes matter consist of twenty-four material elements.

The Sāṃkhya teaching arose in Brahmanic circles. There must therefore have existed in the period of the Upanishads Brahmanic schools which were more occupied with the problem of reincarnation and deliverance from it than with the doctrine of the Brahman. This is the only way to explain how two such completely different forms of thought could develop side by side in Brahmanic circles. It is not impossible that the beginnings of the Sāṃkhya doctrine reach back further than those of the mysticism of identity with the Brahman. Its rise can be better understood, if we assume that the latter was not fully developed or had not yet been disseminated.

Elements of the doctrine are found in the Upanishads. In its main outlines it was probably already established about 550 B.C. It is found systematically worked out in the Sāṃkhyakārikā, a text which belongs to one of the first centuries of our era.

The Sāṃkhya doctrine abandons Brahmanic

monism and addresses itself to a dualistic mode of contemplation. From all eternity, so it assumes, soul-substance and matter each exists on its own account. Through the fact that they enter into connection with each other and then come apart again the living Universe comes into being. The fundamental thought of the system therefore is related to the Greco-oriental Gnosis.

According to the teaching of Sāṃkhya, from all eternity immaterial individual souls (Puruṣas) exist in countless numbers. Puruṣa originally means human being. What, then, induces these immaterial individual souls to enter into connection with matter (Prakṛti)? This is the form which the general and unanswerable question, for what reason does pure Being appear in a material world, takes in the Sāṃkhya system.

Greco-oriental mysticism presumes that soul feels itself drawn to matter by an obscure impulse and to this surrenders. The Sāṃkhya doctrine gives a different explanation. In its opinion, in some way that cannot be further substantiated or understood, souls are destined to enter into connection with matter in order that through this experience they shall become conscious of their absolute and complete independence of it. In Hegel in the same way the spirit has need of the material world in order to arrive within it at the fullest consciousness of itself. But whilst in Hegel it thus attains to full knowledge of its own being, in the Sāṃkhya doctrine it merely becomes sure of its independence of matter.

In order that immaterial souls may enter into connection with it, matter has to emerge from the state of rest and invisibility in which it originally dwells and come as it were into bloom. According to the teaching of Sāṃkhya, matter does not consist of coarse, visible elements alone, but also of those which are fine and invisible. Delicate matter lets the coarse proceed from it and can take it back again into itself. The psychic soul of man, by which he gains knowledge and thinks and wills, belongs entirely to the invisible, finest matter. Alongside of and in addition to his soul of fine matter, man possesses his immaterial soul. But this has no real share in his life.

Following this doctrine, matter is not in its essence imperfect and bad, but contains in itself the possibility of goodness and perfection no less than that of imperfection and evil. There are in it three components, comparable to three strands (Guṇas) in a plait.

The first Guṇa (the Sattva) is what is full of light, goodness and peace; the second (the Rajas) is what is in motion and craves activity ; the third (the Tamas) is darkness and delusion, from which come evil and suffering.

*   *
*

The Sāṃkhya doctrine, then, makes the world consist of countless matter-entities and soul-entities united to each other. Its opinions have much in common with Leibnitz's theory of monads.

The immaterial soul unites with a psychic soul of fine matter. This is imagined as an etherial, invisible and imperishable body. For the Sāṃkhya doctrine asserts the eternity of matter. When a man dies, it is only his body of coarse matter that passes away. His imperishable psychic *ego*, his etherial body, remains united with the immaterial soul and with it enters on one fresh reincarnation after another.

The immortal psychic *ego*, which is described as Liṅga (the word means a distinguishing mark), is the carrier of the Karman. The doctrine of Karman, that is to say of the deed, is contained in the doctrine of reincarnation in so far as re-birth into a lower or higher state must depend on a man's past actions. It is expressed in the most concise form in one of the Upanishads in the phrase, " What a man does, to such an existence he attains ".

The original meaning of Karman is action, work, especially sacred work, act of sacrifice, rite.

The immaterial soul has no part in the experiences of the psychic soul and its Karman. It must indeed accompany it through its successive existences, but as a mere spectator. For the connection of the two to cease, it is necessary for the psychic soul to arrive at the knowledge that the immaterial soul is independent of the psychic soul and of matter. But it only becomes capable of this through freeing itself from all obscure and low desire that is in matter, letting itself be entirely governed by what is pure and luminous in it—the Sattva—and so attaining rest. This end is reached by the practice of Yoga. Asceticism and self-submergence play just as big a part in the teaching of Sāṃkhya as in the mysticism of becoming one with the Brahman.

It is, then, the psychic soul, not—as logic really would demand of the Sāṃkhya doctrine—the immaterial, which becomes conscious of the absolute essential difference between the non-material and the material. But the existence of this knowledge finishes its work when it comes to the immaterial soul. For by reason of it the connection entered into by the immaterial soul and matter comes to an end. The immaterial soul now again exists independently and is found in a state of blessed unconsciousness and rest. The body of coarse material and the etherial body for their part dissolve back again into the invisible primal matter.

When therefore all immaterial souls are freed from their union with matter, then the world will be redeemed and cease to exist. For henceforth all soul-entities and all matter-entities will have returned to their primal original state of rest. Once more there remains only fine, motionless, invisible matter.

The Sāṃkhya doctrine does not go more closely into the way in which the redemption of the world which it presumes is to come about. It would indeed be difficult to make it comprehensible. According to the hypothesis of the doctrine of reincarnation, the return of the sum-total of soul from matter is really impossible.[1]

But the Universe does not come to rest for ever. It is only that a world period has come to an end. Following an unending rhythm, immaterial souls keep on uniting themselves from time to time ever anew with psychic souls, thus each time causing matter to get into motion again and make the coarsely material issue from it.

The Sāṃkhya theory of world periods following

[1] See on this, pp. 51, 52.

on each other gradually came to be adopted by Indian thought in general. It played a great part in late Brahmanism and late Buddhism.

Ethics had no greater importance in the Sāṃkhya teaching than in Brahmanic mysticism.

* * *

In the older period at all events the Sāṃkhya doctrine does not break with Brahmanic mysticism, although it is altogether different from it. It allows the Brahmanic teaching to describe the totality of all individual souls, although these are not thought of as one entity, as the Brahman; and to conceive deliverance from the cycle of re-births as return into the Brahman. It is only concerned to interpret the doctrine of reincarnation and release from it theoretically and in a way to which no objection can be raised. It can acquiesce in the Brahmanic frame although it is unnecessary and does not fit the picture. Brahmanic thought on its part, in so far as it does not wish to confess the Māyā creed, has great interest in making its own the conception of matter so magnificently thought out by the Sāṃkhya doctrine. This conception satisfies the demands of the doctrine of reincarnation far better than does the Brahmanic theory.

The result is that the Sāṃkhya doctrine tolerates beside it the Brahmanic mysticism of becoming one with the Universal Soul, and that Brahmanism upholds Sāṃkhya beliefs in respect of the doctrine of reincarnation, especially with reference to matter and the union with it entered into by the immaterial soul.

This explains how it is that a form of Sāṃkhya doctrine dovetailed into Brahmanic mysticism is for centuries enormously widespread and almost entirely supplants the pure Brahmanic teaching. This popular Sāṃkhya-Brahmanism is found in nearly all the didactic passages of the Mahābhārata epic. It dominates the famous Bhagavad-Gītā. In this the Sāṃkhya doctrine is even mentioned by name by the god Krishṇa. And what Śaṃkara (9th century A.D.) cites as exoteric teaching of the Upanishads is in the main Sāṃkhya-Brahmanism.

But by the side of Sāṃkhya-Brahmanism there was also a pure, quite independent Sāṃkhya doctrine, as we learn from the Sāṃkhyakārikā and the polemics waged by Śaṃkara against the Sāṃkhya doctrine which rejected the idea of the Brahman. It seems to have played a part especially in the first centuries of our era.

The Sāṃkhya doctrine is a wonderful achievement. Rarely in human thought has a theoretical problem been so clearly recognised; rarely has a solution been undertaken and achieved with such clear judgment.

It was only through the teaching of Sāṃkhya that Jainism and Buddhism became possible. They are new varieties of it in which ethics attain a greater importance. Certain ideas drawn from the Sāṃkhya doctrine are the common spiritual property of India. Every villager is familiar with the teaching contained in the three Guṇas.

It is from the Sāṃkhya doctrine that the ideas are derived on which modern theosophy and Rudolph Steiner's Anthroposophia are built up. Just as in the Sāṃkhya system (see pp. 70, 71), so in Steiner the union between the eternal, immaterial soul (he calls it spirit) and the psychic soul ceases to exist when the psychic soul attains to complete purification. Only Steiner gives a fresh interpretation of the Sāṃkhya doctrine by making it ethical and world and life affirming. According to him it is ordained that the eternal soul which enters into terrestrial existence shall accomplish something of value for the Universe

* *

*

CHAPTER V

JAINISM

IT was mainly in theory that the Sāṃkhya doctrine was concerned with the problem of deliverance from re-birth, whereas Jainism[1] and Buddhism attacked the problem in its practical bearings. These were vigorous elemental movements of world and life negation which had their origin in the fact that men were troubled at heart about the problem of liberation from continuous reincarnation.

The movement began, as far as we can judge, in the warrior caste and spread thence to the other castes, including the Brahmins. Men of all classes left their homes and occupations in crowds and roamed about the world as mendicant friars and ascetics in order by renunciation of the world to gain the privilege of not returning to existence.

It is characteristic of the flight from the world of the Jains and Buddhists that monks no longer lived each for himself, but that they formed monastic orders.

World and life negation played no part in the original doctrine of reincarnation, which was only concerned with ethics and religious ceremonies. The doctrine asserted that those who have accomplished

[1] The more correct form is "Jinism", but it has been thought better to retain the usual English spelling.

good works, and for whom the requisite sacrifices have been offered, pass through the moon into celestial bliss, while others are compelled to return to existence on earth.[1]

But in the Upanishads and in the Sāṃkhya doctrine, the doctrine of reincarnation was connected with the idea of world and life negation. The idea of world and life negation arose from the Brahmanic idea of the immaterial World-Soul and man's union with it. Once there, world and life negation seized possession also of the doctrine of re-birth, although this in itself had nothing to do with the doctrine of the World-Soul and union with it. The idea of purification which was naturally contained in the doctrine of reincarnation came to meet world and life negation.

In alliance with the doctrine of reincarnation, the idea of world and life negation which had originated in the mysticism of union with the Brahman first began to develop its full power. It now entered the service of a quite elementary conception of redemption. In Brahmanic mysticism the idea of redemption could not reach full development. It was not really concerned at all—and this one cannot emphasise enough—with winning redemption, but only with the experience of being exalted above the world. According to the Brahmanic doctrine, what is immaterial is in no need whatever of being redeemed from what is material. The immaterial is not imprisoned in matter, but when the material passes away is naturally released from it and returns into the Universal Soul.[2]

[1] For the original primitive doctrine of reincarnation, see pp. 47-50.
[2] On this see also pp. 41, 42 and pp. 49-51.

All mysticism premises the idea that the soul lives in genuine freedom from the world. Mysticism is the realisation, glorification and manifestation of a naturally given state of redemption from the world ; it is not a struggling and striving to attain to that state.

From the time when world and life negation took possession of the doctrine of re-birth the demand for the renunciation of the world derived from it. We know from the Upanishads that many individuals responded to its call. But it was only in the course of the 8th and 7th centuries B.C. that the new conception of reincarnation dominated by world and life negation penetrated to the hearts of the people. Then in the 6th century the fear of reincarnation became a mass experience.

But there is a profound difference between the world and life negation of Brahmanic mysticism and the world and life negation inspired by fear of re-incarnation. The first has no connection with ethics, but is supra-ethical. The world and life negation on the other hand which springs from the longing for deliverance from re-birth, endeavours to be comprehended and justified as ethical. It does not drive ethics from the place they occupy in the doctrine of reincarnation, but approaches them as being itself a kind of supreme ethic which is requisite for real purification.

Not enough notice is taken of the fact that in ancient Indian Thought we are concerned with two kinds of world and life negation—the supra-ethical, which is an end in itself, and a variety which claims to be the highest form of ethics.

It is true there are passages of the Upanishads which speak of release from reincarnation through supra-ethical world and life negation. But if one studies them more closely, one notices that they premise the mysticism of union with the Brahman, and that the idea of reincarnation is brought into connection with this and governed by it. When it is only a question, as in Jainism and with the Buddha, of the problem of deliverance from re-birth, world and life negation does not raise a claim to be above all ethics, but desires to be the supreme ethic.

But the question is whether detachment from the world, as it results from world and life negation, can assume an ethical significance. Is it not in essence supra-ethical ? Is not the detachment from the world demanded by ethics quite a different thing from that which is based on world and life negation as such ?

*   *

*

Like the Sāṃkhya doctrine, Jainism concedes that matter is real ; and like that, too, it assumes a plurality of immaterial individual souls existing from all eternity. But it diverges from it in that it says the immaterial soul is actually affected by the Karman and the experiences of the psychic *ego*. In conformity with this, deliverance from reincarnation must be presented in a different form from that which it takes in the doctrine of Sāṃkhya, namely, in such a way that by purity of conduct the soul cleanses itself from the besmirching it has suffered and altogether frees itself from evil. What is new, then, in Jainism is the importance attained by ethics. The conception of the Brahmins and adherents of Sāṃkhya that redemption is only effected by knowledge is abandoned. The idea of being exalted over the world is replaced by that of keeping pure from the world—an event full of significance for the thought of India !

Jainism comes into the light of history through Mahāvīra, a contemporary of the Buddha. Like the latter he belongs to the warrior caste. The date of his death may be put at about 477 B.C.

The Founder of the system is said to have been Pārśvanātha (8th century B.C. ?). It gets its name from the fact that according to tradition Pārśvanātha and Mahāvīra bore the title of honour " Victor " (Jina), which was also bestowed on the Buddha.

So Jainism is connected with the oldest form of Sāṃkhya doctrine ; much of it indeed is of very ancient character. It has endured down to the present day. The number of its adherents, who belong principally to the merchant class, is now about a million.

Jainism, then, is not confined only to the ethics of tradition, as are the Brahmanic and Sāṃkhya systems, but seeks in addition to give ethical significance to world and life negation. This endeavour explains how in Jainism not to kill and not to harm living creatures (Ahiṃsā) first becomes a great commandment.

The verb *hims* is the desiderative form of *han* (to kill, to damage), so it means to wish to kill and to damage. So the substantive A-hiṃsā means renunciation of the will to kill and to damage.

*   *
*

How can we explain the origin of the Ahiṃsā commandment ?

It does not develop, as one might expect, out of a feeling of compassion. The most ancient Indian thought hardly knows sympathy with the animal creation. It is true that through the Brahmanic idea of Universal Soul it is convinced of the homogeneousness of all created things. But this it retains as purely theoretical knowledge and, incomprehensible as it seems to us, neglects to draw the conclusion that man must have sympathy with the animal creation as with his own kind.[1]

Had it really been sympathy that originated the commandment not to kill and not to harm, it would be impossible to understand how it could set itself these limits and disregard insistence on the giving of real help. The pretext that world and life negation stood in the way is not plausible. At the very least sympathy must have rebelled against the narrowing limitation. But nothing of the kind happened.

The commandment not to kill and not to harm does not arise, then, from a feeling of compassion, but from the idea of keeping undefiled from the world. It belongs originally to the ethic of becoming more perfect, not to the ethic of action. It was for his own sake, not from a fellow-feeling for other beings, that the pious Indian of those ancient days endeavoured very strictly to carry out the principle of non-activity in his relations to living creatures. Violence seemed to him the action that most must be avoided.

It is true that the Ahiṃsā commandment presumes the doctrine of the like nature of all beings. But it does not arise from compassion, but from the general principle of non-activity as it results from Indian

[1] On this, see p. 43.

world and life negation as such.

As Jainism and the Brahmanic system hold in common the belief in the homogeneity of all beings and the principle of world and life denial, the Ahiṃsā commandment may just as well have originated in Jaina as in Brahmanic circles. The latter is generally assumed to be the case, but the former is really more probable. In Jainism Indian world and life negation first assumes an ethical character. And from the very beginning the Jains ascribe great importance to the commandment not to slay and not to harm, whilst in the Upanishads it is only mentioned as it were by the way. In general : how is it credible that the idea of abandoning killing should have arisen among the Brahmins, who practised killing as a profession in the sacrifices ? There is indeed much that points to the Brahmins having adopted the Ahiṃsā commandment from Jainism.

When once the Ahiṃsā commandment has become generally accepted, it operates with educative effect. It arouses compassionate feeling and keeps it awake. As time goes on it is explained as arising from the motive of sympathy and is lauded as being behaviour originating in fellow-feeling. But that it originally arose from the principle of abstention from action is seen by the fact that it keeps within the bounds of compassionate non-activity and completely disregards helpful sympathy.

In the Āyāraṃgasutta, a Jaina text dating probably from the 3rd or 4th century B.C., Ahiṃsā is preached in the following words : [1]

[1] See Winternitz, *History of Indian Literature*, ii. (Calcutta, 1933), p. 436.

"All saints (Arhats) and Lords (Bhagavats) in the past, in the present and in the future, they all say thus, speak thus, announce thus and declare thus: One may not kill, nor ill use, nor insult, nor torment, nor persecute any kind of living being, any kind of creature, any kind of thing having a soul, any kind of beings. That is the pure, eternal, enduring commandment of religion which has been proclaimed by the sages who comprehend the world."[1]

Centuries later, the poet Hemacandra (12th century A.D.), by the desire of King Kumārapāla, who had been converted to Jainism by him, treats of the doctrine which had become dear to the King in a didactic poem, and praises non-killing and non-harming in the splendid verses:
"Ahiṃsā is like a loving mother of all beings.
"Ahiṃsā is like a stream of nectar in the desert Saṃsāra.
"Ahiṃsā is a course of rain-clouds to the forest-fire of suffering.
"The best herb of healing for the beings that are tormented by the disease
"Called the perpetual return of existence is Ahiṃsā."

In accordance with the Ahiṃsā commandment, the Jains give up bloody sacrifices, the use of meat, hunting and wild beast fights. They also make it their duty to be careful not to trample unawares on creeping things and insects as they walk. The Jain monks go so far as to tie a cloth in front of their mouths in order that as they breathe they may not swallow the tiny creatures of the air. Jainism also sees itself forced to abandon field-work because it is impossible to dig up the earth without damaging minute living things. That is why the Jains are mainly engaged in trade.

The laying down of the commandment not to kill and not to damage is one of the greatest events in the

[1] See Winternitz, ii. p. 569.

spiritual history of mankind. Starting from its principle, founded on world and life denial, of abstention from action, ancient Indian thought—and this in a period when in other respects ethics have not progressed very far—reaches the tremendous discovery that ethics know no bounds! So far as we know, this is for the first time clearly expressed by Jainism.

It remains the great merit of Indian thought that it held fast to knowledge imparted to it by a marvellous dispensation of providence and recognised its importance. But it is remarkable that it failed to examine this knowledge from every side and to concern itself with the problem contained in it. Ethics without limits cannot indeed be completely complied with, but Indian thinking did not discuss this fact. It did not admit it at all. In incomprehensible fashion it clung fast to its illusion, as if not-killing and not-harming were completely possible of fulfilment by anyone who takes the matter seriously. Thus the Jains pass by the great problem as if it did not exist.

However seriously man undertakes to abstain from killing and damaging, he cannot entirely avoid it. He is under the law of necessity, which compels him to kill and to damage both with and without his knowledge. In many ways it may happen that by slavish adherence to the commandment not to kill compassion is less served than by breaking it. When the suffering of a living creature cannot be alleviated, it is more ethical to end its life by killing it mercifully than it is to stand aloof. It is more cruel to let domestic animals which one can no longer feed die a painful death by starvation than to give them a quick and painless end by violence. Again and again we see ourselves placed under the necessity of saving one living creature by destroying or damaging another.

The principle of not-killing and not-harming must not aim at being independent, but must be the servant of, and subordinate itself to, compassion. It must therefore enter into practical discussion with reality. True reverence for morality is shown by readiness to face the difficulties contained in it.

If Indian thought were occupied with the whole of ethics, and not merely with the ethics of non-activity, it could not avoid, as it does, nor endeavour to escape, the practical confronting of reality.

But once again, it is just because it simply lays down non-killing and non-harming as a dogma, that it succeeds in preserving safely through the centuries the great ethical thought which is connected with it.

*　　*
*

Chinese ethics also reach the point of studying the problem of man and the animal creation. But here kindness to all creatures is founded on the essential relationship between them and mankind and on natural sympathy. And it is not limited to non-killing and non-harming. Active compassion is commanded.

It is the Kan-Ying-P'ien (the Book of Deeds and their Rewards) that goes furthest in its demands for compassion for animals. It is a popular work which originated about the period of the Sung Dynasty (A.D. 960–1227), that is to say, during the renaissance of Chinese thought, and is at the present day still one of the most widely read works of Chinese literature. It contains a collection of 212 mostly very short sentences about good and evil which are probably much older than the book itself.

There are editions of this book in which every maxim is accompanied by a short explanation and elucidated by several stories.

Commandments of the Kan-Ying-P'ien.—" Have a pitiful heart for all creatures."—" One must bring no sorrow even upon worms and plants and trees."—" He does evil . . . who shoots birds, hunts animals, digs up the larvae of insects, frightens nesting birds, stops up burrows, removes nests, wounds animals with young . . . will not allow man and beast to take their rest."

From the Explanations of the Commandments.—" If one sees animals in need, one must take heed to help them and preserve their lives."

" Do not allow your children to amuse themselves by playing with flies or butterflies or little birds. It is not merely that such proceedings may result in damage to living creatures: they awake in young hearts the inclination to cruelty and murder."

" The heaven and the earth give to all creatures life and growth. If you harm them, you do not imitate the kindness of the heaven and the earth."

Stories to Elucidate the Commandments.—The wife of a soldier named Fan was consumptive and near to death. As a remedy she was ordered to eat the brains of a hundred sparrows. When she saw the birds in a cage, she sighed and said : " Shall it come to pass that to cure me a hundred living creatures shall be slain ? I will rather die than allow that suffering shall come to them." She opened the cage and let them fly. Shortly after, she recovered from her illness.

Tsao-Pin lived in a house that was in ruins. His children besought him to have it repaired. But he answered them : " In the cold of winter the cracks in the walls and the fissures between the roof-tiles and between the stones offer shelter and refuge to all sorts of living things. We ought not to bring them into danger of perishing."

Wu-Tang of Liu-Ling used to take his son out hunting

with him. One day they came across a stag playing with its young. When it saw Tang, it took to flight. But Tang took an arrow and killed the little one. The terrified stag went off with cries of pain. When Tang had hidden in the long grass, the stag returned and licked the young one's wound. Tang again drew his bow and killed it. After a time he saw another stag and let fly an arrow at it. But the arrow glanced from its course and pierced his son. Then Tang threw down his bow and weeping embraced his child. At this moment he heard a voice from the air saying to him : " Tang, the stag loved its young just as much as you loved your son ".

Attempts have been made to explain the ethic of love for all living creatures for which the Kan-Ying-P'ien stands as resulting from influence exercised by the Indian Ahiṃsā commandment on Chinese ethics. This is impossible. It is true that in the first centuries of our era Buddhism was widely spread in China, and in the very form of the Mahāyāna-Buddhism which makes mercifulness to all creatures still more pressing a duty than did the Buddha himself. But nowhere in the Kan-Ying-P'ien does the peculiar nature of the Indian compassion which is entirely based on a world-view of world and life negation make its influence felt. Chinese thought advances independently from the idea of love to mankind as it is found in Confucius (Kung-Tse, 551-479 B.C.), Mi-Tse (d. about 400 B.C.) and Meng-Tse (372-289 B.C.), to that of love to the whole creation. Acquaintance with Buddhism and the Indian commandment of Ahiṃsā must certainly have furthered this development. But already in Meng-Tse, that is to say, long before Buddhism comes to China, we find a far-reaching sympathy with animals. Meng-Tse praises King Suan of Tsi because he takes compassion on an ox destined to be slaughtered in sacrifice when some bells are being dedicated and orders that it shall be released. Such a mentality, he says, should suffice to make a man king of the world.

Individual maxims of the Kan-Ying-P'ien betray

acquaintance with the Indian Ahiṃsā commandment. But the spirit of its ethic of boundless compassion is not Indian. The compassion inculcated by Chinese ethics is not derived from theories but springs from natural feeling. It is not confined within the circle of world and life negation, but requires merciful activity.

* * *

The commandment to abstain from untruthfulness, which occupies the first place in the ethics of the Upanishads (for they give no such great importance to Ahiṃsā), in Jainism holds the second.

The Jaina monk, further, makes it his duty to avoid dishonesty and unchastity and to give up all his possessions.

The commandments of the Jaina system can only be fully carried out by ascetics who renounce the world. These monks, who mainly came from the warrior caste, formed an order. Beside the order was a lay community for whose members the preservation of the sanctity of marriage replaced the commandment of chastity. They might work and earn money, but their hearts should be free from the care of and pleasure in earthly things.

Monks and laymen alike had to preach true freedom from the world by calmly accepting the evil that men did them and suppressing within their hearts all impulses of hate and revenge.

In Jainism, then, world and life negation already assumed a pronouncedly ethical character.

* * *

The belief, too, that man can do nothing whatever to gain deliverance from reincarnation is represented in Indian thought. In an older period it is especially championed by Gosāla, who has the second name Makkhali, a contemporary of Mahāvīra. According to Gosāla, the number of re-births that a man has to go through is determined by fate. "Happiness and sorrow are measured out to him as it were in bushels, and the duration of the transmigration of souls has its fixed term ; there is no shortening and no lengthening of it, no enlargement and no diminution. As a ball of yarn thrown to the ground runs out and rolls up again, just so will fools and wise men alike, by completing the cycle of transmigration, bring about the end of sorrow."

The Buddha opposes Gosāla most vigorously. In one of his sermons he refers to him thus : " As of all woven garments that there are, a hair shirt is said to be the worst—a hair shirt, Disciples, is cold in cold weather, hot in hot weather, dirty in colour, evil-smelling, rough to the touch—so, Disciples, among all the doctrines of other ascetics and Brahmins is the doctrine of Makkhali the worst ".

* * *

CHAPTER VI

THE BUDDHA AND HIS TEACHING

SIDDHĀRTHA, who later bears the name of Buddha, that is to say The Enlightened, was descended from the noble race of Śākyas, whose home was in north-east India. His father ruled in the city of Kapilavastu.

When nine-and-twenty years of age he left wife and child, and as the ascetic Gotama (Gotama is the clan name of the Śākyas) went forth " from home into homelessness ". The thought that all birth leads only to suffering and death, and that the succession of births is endless, had robbed him of all joy in life. He now sought deliverance from reincarnation.

He passed seven years in fasting, mortification of the flesh and exercises in self-submergence. At last he abandoned fasting and mortification of the flesh. Under a peepul-tree (*Ficus religiosa*) near the village of Uruvelā, the present-day Bodh Gayā, to the south of Patna, he experienced the absorption in which the redeeming knowledge (Bodhi) of deliverance from rebirth is imparted.

He remained for many days on the same spot " enjoying the bliss of deliverance " and battling with himself as to whether he might keep the knowledge attained for himself alone or must communicate it to the world, which perhaps would not understand it. When he had resolved on the latter course, he went to Benares, where he preached his first sermon in a grove near the city and won his first disciples in the persons of five monks who were already known to him from earlier times. He founded a monastic order, and gained also many adherents among laymen.

Then for many years he went about teaching. He died at the age of eighty, at Kusinārā, the present Kasiā, in the Gorakhpore district, about the year 485 B.C.

We find the earliest information about the Buddha and his message in the Tripiṭaka (the word means threefold basket), which consists of three collections of texts. The texts of the first basket (Vinayapiṭaka) contain the Rules of the Order, those of the second (Suttapiṭaka) the discourses of the Buddha, those of the third (Abhidhammapiṭaka) treatises on his doctrine.

Part of the Buddha's discourses were probably already fixed in writing as early as the 3rd century B.C., if not even sooner.

The language of these texts is not Sanskrit but Pāli, a dialect of north-east India which had come to be the ecclesiastical language of Buddhism. Its relation to Sanskrit is about the same as that of Italian to Latin.

The Buddha himself preached in the dialect, related to Pāli, of the Magadha country. He instructed his disciples that each should proclaim the doctrine in his own language.

The Milindapañha ("Questions of Milinda") gives an excellent exposition of the Buddha's teaching. Milinda is the Greek prince Menander who ruled over Bactria from 125 to 95 B.C. and extended his empire far into India. Not long after his death, the Indian provinces of the Greco-Bactrian kingdom were lost again.

In the Milindapañha the prince, who seems attached to the Buddhist faith, addresses questions concerning it to the Buddhist monk Nāgasena, who gives him excellent answers.

In its original form the work was probably composed at the beginning of our era. Later on many fresh sections were added to it.

* *
*

The Buddha was a reformer and reminds us of Luther.

In the matter of religion there is a striking similarity between them. Both of them began by struggling with the problem of redemption. Luther was anxious about the question how forgiveness of sins may be attained, and the Buddha about how liberation from the misery of constantly repeated re-birth can be possible.

In their struggle for redemption both were free spirits. They dared to sever connection with the principle of striving after works which dominated the piety of their age. Luther declared that mediaeval Christian justification by works and the monastic life were of no avail for redemption, while the Buddha rejected the asceticism and self-mortification of his time. Both sought to attain redemption by the path of works and both discovered by experience that it does not lead to the goal, and therefore turned their attention to a spiritualised form of religion.

The distinctive feature of the religion of the Buddha consists first of all in his rejection equally with the material enjoyment of life of the asceticism and self-torture practised by Brahmins and the adherents of the Sāṃkhya doctrine and Jainism. Renunciation of the world, he preaches, consists above all in men attaining the inner state of deliverance from things, not so much in their achieving the uttermost renunciation outwardly. He whose spirit is really free from the world can concede their rights to natural needs without becoming worldly. The Buddha was firm in this conviction because of his own experience that he did not attain enlightenment when he mortified and tormented his body, but when he took food again and ceased to be a "self-torturer".

Thus in the world and life negation to which he was devoted, the Buddha kept some measure of naturalness. This is what was great in him. Whilst he mitigated the severity of world renunciation, he made a fresh and great concession to world and life affirmation.

In the same way, Luther, through his own innate naturalness, emancipated himself from the world and life negation of mediaeval Christianity. Only he got further than the Buddha did in world and life affirmation. He dared to say that a man's calling and a man's work are sacred.

Like other ascetics—we learn it from his discourses—the Buddha had tortured himself by never sitting down at all or only sitting on his heels. Like them, he had allowed himself no couch save one covered with thorns. He had eaten the dung of calves and drunk urine. He had wasted to a skeleton through fasting.

There were also ascetics who made a vow to live just like dogs. They went on all fours and only ate what was thrown to them on the ground. In this way they thought they would arrive at being born again as beings resembling the gods. But after his enlightenment the Buddha, mocking them, says that after their death they will have gained by this reincarnation as dogs.

Although he lived as a mendicant friar, after his

enlightenment the Buddha accepted invitations to tastefully prepared meals and permitted his disciples to do the same. For this he was bitterly vituperated by other ascetics.

It is a further characteristic of the Buddha's manner of thought that he quite decisively rejected the Brahmanic doctrine of the Universal Soul and the identity with it of the individual soul. He maintained, and with justice, that it explains neither the continuance of reincarnation nor redemption from it. Therefore he regarded it as a vain invention and opposed it.

In every way, therefore, the Buddha denied the existence of a sole supreme Being. In so far he was an atheist. On the other hand, he did not deny that there are gods. But for him these were only transient beings, like man, only they belong to a higher order than man does. They cannot help man, and man need not serve them.

There were Brahmins also who thought little of the gods and the service of the gods. But their distinction between higher and lower truth enabled them to leave the people their belief. The Buddha on the contrary aimed at freeing the people from the inadequate religious convictions in which they lived.

The Buddha broke with the sacred writings of the Brahmins just as be broke with their doctrine. The four Vedas, the Brāhmaṇas and the Upanishads were nothing to him.

And further, he showed himself a free-thinker in opening his monastic Order even to members of the despised Śūdra castes. To whatever caste a man belongs, he says in one of his discourses, if he live the true life of a monk, he can nevertheless reach perfection. Whether the fire be kindled with costly wood, or with wood from a dog-trough, or from a pig-trough, or from a laundry-trough, or from a castor-oil tree : it has the same flame, the same brightness and the same power of illumination.

But the Buddha's broad-mindedness must not be understood in the sense of his having altogether declared himself for the abolition of caste distinctions. His opinion is that the monks alone, who are leaving behind them all earthly relationships, are no longer subject to them. They are still valid for people who remain in the ordinary life of the world. The thought of reforming society is as far from the Buddha as from St Paul. Both see their vocation only in leading man away out of the earthly and holding up before him the perfection which he ought to reach. The terrestrial world is for them something doomed to pass away. To trouble about the improvement of worldly conditions seems to them as little opportune as to undertake repairs in a house that is about to be pulled down. That is why the Buddha does not attack the validity of the caste distinctions in ordinary life ; and why Paul is not led by the principle of Christian love to demand the abolition of slavery.

It is only with the permission of their masters that slaves may enter the Order founded by the Buddha. Similarly, the permission of their parents is necessary for all young people, to whatever caste they may belong.

It is also an important achievement that the Buddha grants to women the right to the monastic life and founds an Order of nuns. He reaches this resolution indeed only after long opposition and only at the intercession of his favourite disciple, Ānanda. The prerogatives of monks in relation to nuns are fully upheld. According to a rule ascribed to the

Buddha, a nun, even if she has been ordained for a hundred years, must salute every monk in the most reverential manner, even if he has only just joined the Order, must remain standing in his presence, raise folded hands and show him due honour.

To his question why in public life women are not given the same rank and the same rights as men, Ānanda receives from the Master the reply : " Women, Ānanda, are hot-tempered ; women, Ānanda, are jealous ; women, Ānanda, are envious ; women, Ānanda, are stupid ".
Another of the Buddha's sayings is : " Crying is the power of the child ; anger is the power of women ".

* *
*

The most revolutionary of the Buddha's proceedings is that, in order to break completely with the Brahmanic doctrine of redemption, he altogether disputes that the transitory world of the senses is in any way based on eternal, supra-sensuous Being. He denies therefore not alone the existence of the Universal Soul, but also that of the individual soul. To establish this, he sets up two fundamental principles for the investigation of truth. The spirit should only be occupied with what has direct practical significance for redemption : only what results from direct evidence may be regarded as fact.

In obedience to the first principle he forbids his disciples to aim at the attainment of complete knowledge of the world. He regards as useless investigation into the nature of Being and appearances, and the disputations so much held in his time about dogmatic opinions.

A disciple who criticises him for passing over so many questions is answered with a parable. If a man, says the Buddha, is struck by a poisoned arrow, he does not wait to have the wound treated until he knows whether it was a nobleman, or a Brahmin, or a Vaiśya or a Śūdra who shot him, nor until he has investigated what the man's name is, to what family he belongs, whether he is tall or short or of medium stature, and what the weapon he made use of looks like. If he were to act thus, he would die of his wound. He can only be saved if he immediately entrusts himself to the doctor summoned by his relations and friends.

In particular, one should not worry about the questions whether the world is eternal or transitory, whether it is finite or infinite, whether life and body are one and the same or not one and the same, and whether the "perfected one" (that is to say redeemed) still exists after death or no longer exists. About these and similar problems the Buddha will give no information, because knowledge of them is not necessary to the attainment of redemption.

But what then, according to the Buddha, can and must a man know?

First of all he must recognise the fact that in the terrestrial world there is no real joy, but that all life is suffering. In his first sermon at Benares, the Buddha announces the "noble truth about suffering" in these words: "Birth is suffering, old age is suffering, death is suffering, to be united with what one loves not is suffering, to be separated from what one loves is suffering, not to attain one's desires is suffering".

Profounder and more true than this one-sided, pessimistic view of life is that held by the Brahmins. They allow earthly existence to be made up of pleasure and pain, but regard both as vanity. Whoever has experienced union with the Universal Soul is exalted over pleasure and pain alike. But even in the Upanishads we find sayings which make transitory and sorrowful simply equivalent, just as the Buddha does. Thus a great exposition of the doctrine of the Brahman in the Upanishads closes with the words: " What is different from it (the Brahman) is full of sorrow ".

But according to the Buddha, we must not only realise that this life on earth is full of sorrow, but also that this existence is our lot because, under the delusion that it can bring us pleasure, we cherish desire for it. It is the meaningless will-to-live—the Buddha calls it the desire for existence and pleasure—that leads living beings from reincarnation to reincarnation. The end of suffering can only be brought about by men killing in themselves the will-to-live. If they do this, they arrive at not being born again any more and enter into Nirvāṇa.

The Buddha therefore does not explain deliverance from transmigration, as do the Brahmins, the Sāṃkhya doctrine and Jainism, as the liberation of the soul from the world of the senses, but, apparently more simply, as a complete cessation of life which is attained by direct renunciation of the will-to-live.

He argues that, if one holds to the principle that only what results from direct evidence may be regarded as fact, our knowledge of the Universe shrinks to quite a little. We know only of "formations" (Saṃkhāras), that is of happenings which are enacted in corporeal phenomena. And, further, we can establish the fact that in what happens there rules a necessity determined by law. One manifested event results from another and follows upon it. And finally it can be asserted with confidence that all events can be referred back to will-to-be and would not occur without it.

The Buddha maintains that everything happens in the world in conformity with necessity governed by law, in opposition to the Brahmins, who contemplate all that happens in the Universe as a game without any rules. But he does not adopt the principle of causality from any kind of insight into natural science, but because of his conception of Karman. If the deeds of men work themselves out through countless existences in good or bad forms of reincarnation as determined by their nature, then, he quite rightly deduces, the law of cause and effect must dominate the whole of what happens in the Universe.

And, further, the psychic *ego*, according to the Buddha, is not an enduring self. The events and actions which fill a man's life in his view form as it were only an outward sequence borne on by a constantly renewed will-to-live.

As narrated in the Milindapañha, the Buddhist monk who offers to carry on a debate with King Milinda replies to the King's question as to what his name is that he is called Nāgasena. But, he at once adds, this is a mere name. A real *ego* corresponding to him is only apparently present. And he proceeds to explain this assertion to the astonished King by a metaphor. As the flame from a wick, he says, is in reality only a constant succession of flames which, seen as a unity, keep on rising from the same inflammable material, so that which we regard as our *ego* is something which is constantly being formed anew in the succession of events which constitute our existence.

But the Buddha cannot really make plausible this denial of the spiritual *ego* for which he is so eager. Ethics and the Karman doctrine will not allow it. It is only when the *ego* is in some way a permanent thing that retains its identity and therefore in some way possesses reality, that it is capable of ethical reflection and behaviour, and definitely can be so by means of the Karman of its earlier existences. In his practical teaching, then, the Buddha can make no use of his theoretical conception of Being, and he does not attempt to.

In general, he does not succeed in freeing the doctrine of the cycle of re-births and liberation from it from the idea, which was originally connected with it, of a transcendental Being, nor does he succeed in fitting it into his purely empirical method of regarding things. Again and again it happens that he swerves aside from his theory that redemption is a cessation of existence, and expresses himself in such a way that, as in the Sāṃkhya doctrine and in Jainism, it can be understood as eternal, blissful rest.

What are we to understand by Nirvāṇa?

Nirvāṇa means extinction. The word is used even before the Buddha. It comes into use in Jainism. The Jaina system—as also the Sāṃkhya system—cannot apprehend blessedness as an absorption of the individual soul into the Universal Soul, but must imagine it as an eternal coming-to-rest of the individual soul as such. The word Nirvāṇa probably arose as an expression for this blessed state of the individual soul in which it has lost the consciousness of itself. Then later on the Brahmins took it over and used it also for the merging of the individual soul in the Universal.

To the question, how one can talk of the bliss of Nirvāṇa,

seeing that there is no feeling there, Sāriputta, one of the Buddha's favourite disciples, replies: "Just that, my friend, is bliss, that there is no feeling there".

And finally it is said of Nirvāṇa, that exact knowledge of it is unnecessary.

In order completely to refute the Brahmins, the Buddha denies that material being is in any way founded on immaterial, but does so without being able really to argue this out. It would have been simpler for him to renounce knowledge of Being altogether and be satisfied with the established fact that all life in the sensuous world is suffering, leaving on one side the question in how far there is a spiritual Being which corresponds to the coming into and passing out of existence of this world of the senses.

In recent times doubts have been expressed from many directions as to whether the denial of the reality of immaterial Being and of the psychic *ego* actually belonged at all to the original teaching of the Buddha.

* *
*

The significance of the Buddha does not lie in the domain of theoretic thought, but in the fact that he spiritualises world and life negation and breathes into it a breath of ethics. He makes his own the ethical acquisitions of Jainism and carries further what was there begun.

Because the Buddha preaches that all life is sorrowful he has been held—before there was any accurate knowledge of Jainism—to be the creator of the ethic of compassion, and it has been believed that the commandment not to kill and not to damage originated from him. This is not true. He found the Ahiṃsā commandment in Jainism and adopted it from that source.

The Ahiṃsā commandment does not appear to be so strictly observed in the more ancient Buddhism as it is in Jainism. The eating of meat was not completely prohibited Otherwise it would have been impossible to relate in the sacred writings of Buddhism that the Buddha died after eating a dish of wild-boar's flesh served to him by the smith, Cunda. It is European scholars who are first scandalised at this account, and try to make it seem probable that the word in question (*sūkaramaddavam*) does not necessarily mean a dish of wild-boar meat, but that we may also understand by the word a meal prepared from herbs, roots or fungi which had a name in which the word wild-boar occurred.

But we know from a saying of the Buddha, or a saying ascribed to him as far back as the most ancient period, that in certain cases, he regarded the eating of flesh as permissible. A court surgeon named Jīvaka, so we are told in the Buddha's discourses, has heard that the Master on occasions even eats meat and therefore questions him about it. Thereupon the Buddha explains to him that he refuses meat when he knows that the animal was slaughtered on purpose for him, but that he allows himself the enjoyment of that placed before him when he happens just to arrive at the time of a meal, or of what is put in his alms-bowl. For the animal was not killed on his account. Therefore he may regard such meat as " blameless nourishment ".

In the same manner, Paul, in the 8th Chapter of the First Epistle to the Corinthians, solves the question whether Christians may eat of the meat from heathen sacrifices. He decides that if one is told that this is its origin, one should not eat of it, for this would be a sin. But if meat is served when heathens invite one to a meal, or if one buys meat in the market, one need not inquire about its origin and can eat it without troubling.

The fact that the sophistical discrimination between slaughter of which one is guilty and slaughter of which one is innocent is made by the Buddha, or can be attributed to him, shows that the older Buddhism was not yet quite strict about the prohibition of meat-eating. The Buddhist monks in Ceylon still keep to this tradition. If meat be placed in their alms-bowls, they eat it.

The Buddha does not bid his disciples bind a cloth before their mouths so that they may breathe in no living things. And he has no objection to agriculture. So he does not pursue the Ahiṃsā commandment as far into details as do the Jains. He is not yet fully conscious of the problem of the boundlessness of ethics.

*　*　*

But even if the commandment not to kill and not to hurt does not begin with the Buddha, he is nevertheless the originator of the ethic of compassion. For he it is who undertook to base on compassion this commandment which originally sprang from the idea of non-activity and keeping unpolluted from the world.

In a discourse he describes in moving words how the thralls and hirelings receive from the king, who wants to organise a great sacrifice, an order to fetch the animals selected for slaughter, and how they set about carrying it out " from fear of punishment, cowed down by fear, their eyes filled with tears ".

It is said that the representations of the silk-weavers that in order to get silk they had to be guilty of the lives of so many little creatures was the reason why he forbade his monks the use of silk coverings.

But the Buddha's ethic of compassion is incomplete. It is limited by world and life negation. Nowhere does the Master demand that because all life is suffering man should strive, in so far as is possible, to bring help to every human being and to every living thing. He only commands the avoidance of pitiless actions. Of sympathetic helping he takes no account. It is excluded by the principle of non-activity which derives from world and life negation.

And in the Buddha it is not merely the principle of non-activity, but the conception of the nature of suffering and deliverance from suffering which goes together with world and life negation that is opposed to compassionate action. If all suffering has its origin in will-to-live, it can only be ended by the denial of that, that is to say only through an act of knowledge by the living creature concerning itself. It is really purposeless to wish to alleviate its sufferings in detail or from without. The fundamental cause of the suffering continues and immediately works itself out anew.

Through world and life negation, compassion loses

its object. It compels man—if he dare to admit it—to regard as purposeless, and to give up, the endeavour to bring help to the life that is in need of it.

And as a matter of fact the Buddha's compassion consists principally in a constant realisation of the fact that all living creatures are for evermore subject to suffering. It is a compassion of the understanding rather than the direct sympathy of the heart which carries within it the impulse to help.

In the more ancient tradition we are not told that the Buddha spoke lovingly of animals and stood towards them in a relationship of the heart. He was no Francis of Assisi.

It is first in the Jātakas, in the legendary stories of his earlier existences, that he is described as the great friend of animals. One of the best known of these stories relates that he gave himself to a hungry tigress to save her from the crime of devouring her own young.

* * *

Because there is no question of action, ethics in the system of the Buddha can only develop as an ethic of thoughts.

If Jainism requires that the monk should suppress all emotions of hatred and revenge, the Buddha lays on him the further command, that he shall meet all living things, yea, the whole Universe, with a feeling of kindness.

" Now this is what you must practise well, my monks : our tempers must remain unruffled, no evil sound shall issue from our lips, we will remain friendly and sympathetic, in a temper of loving-kindness, without secret malice : and we will irradiate our personality with loving feelings ; starting thence we will then . . . irradiate the whole world with broad, deep, unlimited feeling, free from wrath and rancour. This is what you must practise well, my friends." [1]

"Abiding in a spirit of loving-kindness, he (the monk) shines in one direction, then in a second, then in a third, then in a fourth, similarly upward and downward : recognising himself everywhere in everything he irradiates the whole universe with loving-kindness." [2]

For the Brahmins and in the Sāṃkhya doctrine ethics have only the importance that they confer a better reincarnation ; in Jainism they help towards restoring to the soul its original purity ; with the Buddha—and this is what is new—an ethical disposition is requisite for attaining to true self-submergence. If one cares to measure the distance traversed, one must first read portions of the finest discourses of the Buddha and then take up the Upanishads.

With the Buddha meditation comprehends also exercises in ethical thinking. Only he who has a pure mind and in addition is filled with sentiments of cheerful kindness for the whole world is said to be capable of experiencing the highest detachment from the world in self-submergence.

Ecstasy and exercises in self-submergence play no less a part in the system of the Buddha than they do among the Brahmins and adherents of the Sāṃkhya and Jaina systems. He distinguishes four " stages ".

[1] Neumann, *Reden Buddhas*, i. 215.
[2] *Ibid.*, i. 447.
[Direct English translations of these passages may be found in *Further Dialogues of the Buddha*, Majjhima Nikāya : Lord Robert Chalmers. 1926.—Translator's note.]

In the last and highest a man becomes certain that henceforward he will pass through no more reincarnations. Through this certainty he really already enters Nirvāṇa, even if his bodily existence does not yet immediately cease.

In the highest stage he can attain to recollection of his earlier forms of existence, even those in earlier ages of the Universe. The Buddha declares that such an experience has been his.

* * *

But according to the Buddha, the ethical disposition of the mind or spirit has not merely importance for the man himself, but is at the same time a power which goes forth from him. The Buddha possesses this force in unique degree. It constitutes the secret of his powerful and simple personality.

The "radiation of kindliness" issuing from him is said to have affected not only human beings but also animals. A wild elephant which his hostile cousin Devadatta let loose on him in a narrow lane stopped in its course, so the story relates, struck by the force of his kindness, and lowered the trunk it had already raised to strike.

The Buddha is the first to express the fundamental law that ethical spirit quite simply in itself means energy which brings about what is ethical in the world.

From the power of the spirit which is united with it, the Word derives the power to accomplish something.

According to the Buddha it is proper to the

monastic calling in silence and in speech to accomplish good which proceeds from pure and kindly feeling.

" The monk speaks the truth, he is devoted to the truth, steadfast, worthy of confidence, no worldly hypocrite and flatterer. He has renounced back-biting, from back-biting he keeps himself afar. What he has heard here he does not repeat there to set those at variance, and what he has heard there he does not repeat here to set these at variance. Thus he unites the estranged, makes fast those already bound together; harmony makes him happy, harmony delights him, harmony rejoices his heart, he utters words that promote harmony . . . words free from opprobrium, that do good to the ear, rich in love, penetrating to the heart, courteous, delighting many, uplifting many, such words does he speak." [1]

One must endure enmity and forgive evil, not only for the sake of the perfection that is to be attained, but also because in this way something is accomplished in the world. " By non-anger ", says the Buddha, " let anger be overcome; let the evil be overcome with good; let the avaricious man be overcome with gifts; let the liar be overcome with truth; through non-enmity enmity comes to rest."

St Paul says the same: " Be not overcome of evil, but overcome evil with good " (Epistle to the Romans, xii. 21).

The story of Prince Dīghāvu (Livelong), related by the Buddha to his disciples when strife breaks out among them, treats of the enmity which comes to rest through non-enmity. King Brahmadatta has taken the kingdom from his neighbour King Dīghīti (Sufferlong). Later on the

[1] Neumann, *Reden Buddhas*, i. 423-424.

latter lives with his wife, unknown, disguised as a mendicant friar, in the city of his enemy, where a son is born to him, to whom he gives the name Dīghāvu (Livelong). Some years later King Brahmadatta learns through a traitor who the mendicant friar is and has him and his wife executed. As he goes to his death he talks to his son Dīghāvu of the enmity which must be brought to rest by non-enmity. Unknown, Dīghāvu enters the service of the King and gains his friendship. Out hunting he manages one day to arrange that he is quite alone with him in the forest. The weary King lays his head on his lap and falls asleep. Now Dīghāvu judges the moment has come to take revenge. Three times he brandishes his sword over the sleeper's head; three times he lets it sink because the last words of his father come into his mind. But the King dreams that Dīghāvu wants to murder him. Terrified, he starts up, sees Dīghāvu before him with the sword in his hand, and learns from him who he is. Falling down before him, he begs for his life. But Dīghāvu discloses that in obedience to his father's words he must forgive him, and he, for his part, begs the King to forgive him for wanting to kill him. So the enmity finds an end. Dīghāvu is reinstated by the King in his father's dominion.

* *
*

When the Buddha values ethical feeling as such, or as preached in words, as a force operating on the world, he quits the ethic of world and life negation which makes a man only preoccupied with himself. But the ethic of action in the spirit of love nevertheless remains outside the circle of his vision. It is only what is spiritual in the world that he wants to alter, not earthly conditions. It does not occur to him to abandon the principle of non-activity, although the thought of action is already present in his ethics.

He, the acute investigator of the theory of knowledge, passes by the elementary problem whether ethics can really be limited to non-activity, or whether they must not also enter the domain of action, as if he were smitten with blindness. World and life negation is a solid certainty for him as a matter of course. He is unconscious that compassion means a protest against it coming from the very depths of human nature.

When he describes the "righteousness of the monk" in the splendid sentence: "He is sympathetic and merciful, and strives with friendly feeling for the good of all living things", he is far from expecting that the monk will have active love. He merely makes it his duty to possess the kindly disposition which belongs to perfection and true peace of soul.

He teaches that he who follows the sacred eightfold path of right knowledge, right feeling, right speech, right action, right living, right effort, right insight, right meditation attains redemption. But we must not let ourselves be deceived by the phrase "right action". By this he only understands the avoidance of evil.

"What now, my brethren, is right action? To avoid killing what is alive, to avoid taking what is not given, to avoid licentiousness: this, my brethren, is called right action." (From a discourse of Sāriputta, a favourite disciple of the Buddha, on the eightfold path.)

For the Buddha's monks there can be no question of active love, if for no other reason, because it assumes that one loves something in the world and so in some way gives one's heart to it. But this would mean a limitation of freedom from earthly cares. How pathetic is the Buddha's saying : " Those who love nothing in the world are rich in joy and free from pain ". To a father who has lost his little boy, he knows nothing better to say than : " What one loves brings woe and lamentation ".

He draws the ideal of monastic perfection with hard lines in the saying : " He who cares not for others, who has no relations, who controls himself, who is firmly fixed in the heart of truth, in whom the fundamental evils are extinguished, who has thrown hatred from him : him I call a Brahmin ".

* *
*

It is easy to understand how for the sake of the world and life negation which he upholds as the highest law, the Buddha forgoes expecting from his monks activity proceeding from compassion and love. But in his system of ethics for the laity he is faced by the necessity of deciding whether he shall make this a duty or not. If he concedes to men that they may continue to live a life of activity—a thing which is really irreconcilable with his doctrine of suffering and deliverance from suffering—he really ought also to bid them to act with compassion and love. But this would mean such a concession to world and life affirmation as would make an end of world and life denial.

In the Buddha the ethical is so strongly developed that it is already an end in itself. He does not admit this, but leaves ethics still in the service of the redemption dominated by **world and life negation**.

Ethical world and life negation is in itself a contradictory and non-realisable idea. For ethics comprise world and life affirmation. What is regarded as ethical world and life negation is never more than ethics kept within the bounds of world and life negation and is correspondingly incomplete.

So it cannot be otherwise: even the Buddha's ethics for laymen are dominated by world and life negation. They can uphold some of the demands of the ethic of deeds, but can never raise ethical action to a commandment in the all-embracing measure which compassion and love really demand.

It is but seldom that the Buddha speaks at any length on lay ethics. His discourses are ordinarily addressed to monks.

From a Discourse on Ethics for the Laity.[1]—" But I will tell you also, what should be the manner of life for the father of a household . . . seeing that for him, with wife and child, to follow at all the commandments for monks is a thing unattainable. . . . He must kill no living creature; he must not take what is not given to him; he must not lie, he must not drink intoxicating liquor; he must refrain from unchastity . . . as duty bids he must care for his parents and pursue a virtuous and righteous calling."

Further the Buddha lays on the laity the command to practise: liberality, good conduct of life, loving care for relations, blameless acts, reverence and modesty, patience and gentleness, contentment and gratitude, seasonable attendance at instructive discourses, the receiving of visits from ascetics.

The inscriptions carved on stone of the Buddhist King Aśoka (3rd century B.C.) specially recommend to the laity,

---

[1] Suttanipāta, 385–404 (Winternitz, *Der ältere Buddhismus*, p. 81).

besides the observance of the Ahiṃsā commandment, a benevolent attitude to slaves and servants, respect for persons deserving of honour and liberality to Brahmins and ascetics.

The Dhammapada (The Path of Truth), the classical book of ancient Buddhist ethics—it belongs to the Suttapiṭaka, the second " basket " of the sacred writings of the older Buddhism and contains authentic sayings of the Buddha and others that are attributed to him—contains hardly anything about ethics for the laity.

The Buddha's lay ethics disappoint us, then, in so far as they omit to promote action due to the compelling force of compassion and love. A corresponding ethic of action should range itself alongside the magnificent theoretical ethic of compassion and kindness. It is wanting.

Observe : not a word of the aid due to the suffering in their need ! When the Buddha speaks of charity, he means liberality to monks ! He sings the praises of the reward which follows on this in a way which for us is a stumbling-block.

He lays great value on gratitude. In one of his finest discourses he speaks of it as follows : " The sum of all that makes a bad man is ingratitude . . . the sum of all that makes a good man is gratitude ".

On Gratitude to Parents.[1]—" If a man . . . should live to be a hundred years old carrying around his mother on one shoulder and his father on the other . . . he has not even yet rendered thanks to his parents and requited their kindness. . . .

" But he who brings his parents, if they be unbelievers, to perfect faith . . . who brings them, if they be wicked, to perfect virtue . . . brings them, if they be covetous, to

---

[1] Anguttara-Nikaya, ii. 4, 1 ff.

perfect willingness for sacrifice . . . brings them, if they be not wise, to perfect wisdom : such a man has in this way alone rendered thanks to his parents, and requited their kindness, yea, more than requited."

The Buddha's ethics are different from the ethics of Jesus in that he did not demand real active love. Jesus and the Buddha have this in common, that their form of ethics, because it is under the influence of world and life negation, is not an ethic of action but an ethic of inner perfection. But in both the ethic of inner perfection is governed by the principle of love. It therefore carries within it the tendency to express itself in action and in this way has a certain affinity with world and life affirmation. With Jesus the ethic of the perfecting of the self commands active love : with the Buddha it does not get so far.

It must be noted that the world and life negation of Jesus is in origin and in essence quite different from that of the Buddha. It does not rest on the distinction between material and immaterial Being, but abandons the natural world as evil, in the expectation that it will be transformed into a world that is supernatural and good. The world and life negation of Jesus is conditioned by ethics.

Because of this fundamental difference in world and life negation the constantly renewed attempt to explain the teaching of Jesus as derived from Buddhist influences must be pronounced hopeless, even on the altogether improbable assumption that Jesus was acquainted with Indian thought.

Naturally the Buddhist laity, when it seems to be their duty, assume the right of following the natural inclinations of their hearts and practising active love, without worrying about whether it is compatible with world and life negation.

Digging wells and building rest-houses for travellers belong from time immemorial to the good works they practise.

In the commandments, chiselled in stone, of King Aśoka active compassion already begins to play a certain part.

* * *

There are cases also in which the Buddha in person allowed himself to be carried away, and acted from the motive of love. One evening, making a round of the sleeping-quarters, he found a monk suffering from dysentery and, already enfeebled by it, lying in his filth. With the help of his companion Ānanda, he washed him and changed his bed. Afterwards he called the monks together and instructed them as to the help they owed to each other. But he did not base this service on a general commandment of loving activity, but explained that as they had neither father nor mother with them to look after them they must replace father and mother for each other. The exhortation ended with the sentence: " Whoever, monks, would nurse me, he shall nurse the sick man ".

In the personality of the Buddha, so great in its humanity, ethics are so strong and so living that they really find no place in the inactivity demanded by world and life negation. But they do not revolt against it and shatter it, but, wherever occasion offers, as is the natural result, go beyond it, just as pent-in water overflows the dam at one spot and another.

The Buddha says nothing about the question of the redemption of the world. Really we should expect him to voice the hope that in time all living creatures will enter Nirvāna and that in this way the sorrowful process of coming and going will some day quite come to an end. But he takes into account the difficulty of imagining the world-Nirvāna if, in accordance with the hypothesis of the doctrine of reincarnation, all being can only attain redemption by the circuitous route of a human existence capable of the highest knowledge.[1]

According to the Buddha, it already borders on the impossible that a human being who, as a result of evil-doing, enters into a non-human form of existence should later be born again in human form, "because in the low forms of existence there is mutual murder and no good action". If a yoke with one opening be thrown into the sea and in the sea there is a one-eyed turtle which only rises to the surface once in every hundred years, there is much more probability, according to a parable of the Buddha, that this turtle will one day put its neck into this yoke than that the fool who has once sunk to low forms of existence will again attain to human existence.

The fact that the Buddha, the preacher of compassion, makes man only occupied with his own redemption, not with that of all living creatures, is a weakness of his teaching.

*   *
*

For us Europeans—and for modern Indians no

[1] See on this, pp 51, 52, 71-72.

less—there is a certain difficulty in visualising the historical Buddha and his teaching as they really were. We cannot reconcile ourselves to the fact that the great teacher of compassion in theory was still so completely governed by world and life negation and the principle of non-activity which results from it. This will not fit into the ideal portrait which we should like to paint of him. It gives to his character some quality which seems alien to us. And his ethics trouble us because they are incomplete.

With the Buddha we have a similar experience to that we pass through when we study Jesus. It is difficult for us to admit that the thought and ethics of Jesus were influenced by a longing expectation of the end of the world.

But we have sufficient reliable information to compel us to see both teachers as they really were.

The importance of the Buddha consists in his having undertaken to spiritualise world and life negation and make it ethical. He spiritualised it by teaching men to regard the detachment of the heart from material things as more important than the renunciation of the world in actual practice. At the same time he required of his disciples that their inward emancipation from the world should be outwardly expressed in ethical conduct.

Because his thinking was dominated by world and life negation it followed that for him the ethic of active help did not come under consideration. So he was obliged to take no account of this exoteric ethic and could only concern himself with the esoteric ethic of that disposition free from hatred, peaceable and kind, which it is man's duty to strive to acquire and to put to the proof in his dealings with his fellows. Thus he became the creator of the ethic of inner perfection. In this sphere he gave expression to truths of everlasting value and advanced the ethics, not of India alone, but of humanity. He was one of the greatest ethical men of genius ever bestowed upon the world.

But how did it come about that in the Buddha world and life negation became ethical ? Is it really the case, as he himself thought, that world and life negation created for itself an ethic ? In this he was wrong.

World and life negation cannot become anything else than what it essentially is, namely a state of exaltation above the world and indifference towards the world. Ethics can never derive from it. The ethical premises the taking of interest in the welfare of beings that belong to this world, and this regard for terrestrial affairs points to world and life affirmation, however slight the tendency towards it may be.

Ethical world and life negation therefore can never arise through the production of an ethic in conformity with itself, but can only come into being when ethics find expression in world and life negation. This is what happened with the Buddha. With him ethics appeared in Indian world and life negation, just as with Jesus ethics found expression within the late-Jewish world and life negation connected with the expectation of the end of the world.

The Buddha thought he could combine ethics and world and life negation, but in reality he became through ethics untrue to world and life negation, which still dominated him. His ethic of becoming perfect in heart, although it was kept well within the limits of world and life negation, was nevertheless different from this in spirit. The inner freedom from the world which is required by ethics may resemble the freedom which ensues from world and life negation, but in its essence it is a different thing.[1] It originates from the need of greater ethical perfection. The freedom from the world which accompanies world and life negation as such aims at nothing, but is its own end in itself. How clearly did the ancient Brahmins see in this matter, when they maintained that world and life negation is something only concerned with itself, and regarded ethics as belonging to world and life affirmation!

The ethic of the higher inward perfection is not based on world and life negation, but is actually the very core of ethics. The ethic which is adjusted to world and life affirmation must also urge man to strive to become more perfect of heart, a state which is only attainable through inward freedom from the world. But to arrive at this freedom from the world it is not necessary that man should regard the world as unreal. He can recognise significance in earthly things. The profoundest inner freedom from the world is that which man strives to attain in order to become an ethical personality and as such to serve the world.

The Buddha, then, inserts the ethical idea of freedom from the world into world and life negation. He thinks he is giving an ethical sense to world and life-denying inner freedom from the world. But in reality he makes the essentially different idea of

[1] On this question, see also pp. 73, 74.

ethical freedom from the world take the place of that.

As a matter of fact, his ethic of becoming more perfect in heart is an alien element introduced into world and life negation and is prejudicial to it.

Then, in his ethic of compassion, his divergence from world and life negation becomes completely manifest. This form of ethics assumes so developed an interest in terrestrial affairs, and has within itself such strong instincts towards activity, that it is incomprehensible how the Buddha could think it could be combined with the principle of non-activity contained in world and life negation.

Ethics are the secret ally of world and life affirmation, and the Buddha allowed this dangerous enemy to enter the fortress of world and life negation.

He gave to India something it did not yet possess : an ethic derived from thought. Up to then it only knew a traditional morality of virtues and duties, and such an ethic as that is only capable of development up to a certain point. The ultimate higher evolution of ethics only starts when thought begins to be occupied with morals and to seek the fundamental principle which comprehends all virtues and all duties. When the Buddha exalted compassionate love to be the fundamental principle of morality, he breathed into Indian ethics a new breath of life.

He sowed the seed of ethics on the field of world and life negation, but the wind carried some of the seed on to other land. In the course of the centuries there ripened in the popular thought, which was little or not at all affected by the dogma of world and life negation, a magnificent harvest grown from the seed of his ethical ideas.

But this higher evolution of ethics was to the advantage, not of world and life negation, but of world and life affirmation. Through the ethic which he spread, the Buddha gave to the world and life affirmation present in the Indian spirit weapons with which to overcome world and life negation. Without the influence of his ethic the higher evolution which took place in Hinduism in the centuries which followed would be unthinkable. Through the ethic which originated with the Buddha, Hinduism gained the strength to make an end of Buddhism in India.

After long hesitation the spirit of India was obliged in the main to reject the Buddha's world and life negation. But it kept his ethic.

* *
*

CHAPTER VII

LATER BUDDHISM IN INDIA

FROM some words addressed to Ānanda we know that the Buddha anticipated that the truth he preached would endure only 500 years. Then there must be a fresh revelation of redemption.

This prophecy was not fulfilled. Five hundred years after the Buddha's death, that is to say about the beginning of our era, his doctrine was approaching the height of its flowering season. It is true it was no longer quite the same as he preached it, for it had gone on developing.

In later Buddhism there evolved the belief that from time immemorial the truth leading to redemption has been proclaimed by Buddhas. Gotama Buddha of the Śākhya race is thus only one among many. In every world period—later Buddhism adopts from the Sāṃkhya system the conception of successive world periods—and in every part of the Universe (that is to say, not only on the earth) from time to time Buddhas make their appearance. Gotama Buddha is not the last. Others will follow him.

According to late Buddhist doctrine, all the Buddhas derive from a heavenly, self-created Proto-Buddha (Ādi-Buddha) from whom the Universe also has its origin. Among the eternal Buddhas whose descent is directly traceable from him, Buddha-Amitābha (he of immeasurable light), the protector of the present world, is preeminent. His dwelling-place is the world of Paradise, Sukhāvatī. The dogmatics of late Buddhism made Gotama Buddha also a heavenly being who took on him the form of a man in order to bring knowledge of redemption to the world. In individual writings of the period he was even described, like the Proto-Buddha, as "the self-created Father of the Universe". The later Buddhist doctrine of Buddhas was not developed consistently, but contains many obscurities and contradictions.

So later Buddhism became a religion. And it was not contented with merely sanctioning the adoration of Buddhas, but brought about the revival of the worship of the gods in general, to which Gotama Buddha had denied all importance.

Whilst it thus developed into a popular religion, later Buddhism wandered far from the doctrine of the historical Buddha that deliverance from reincarnation can only be attained by the monastic life and renunciation of the world. It asserted that those who remain in ordinary life also share in redemption, if in faith they venerate the divine Buddha and confidently dedicate themselves to him.

This new teaching, which announced a way of redemption which all can enter and more easily follow, is called the doctrine of the " big vessel " (Mahāyāna). The original doctrine derived from the historical Buddha is described as that of the " small vessel " (Hīnayāna). By this is meant the vessel which conveys men across the stream of re-birth and suffering to the shore of Nirvāna.

*   *
*

Mahāyāna-Buddhism also went beyond the teaching of the historical Buddha in that it no longer regarded liberation from reincarnation as the highest goal to be aimed at. The idea of compassion was so strongly developed in it that it became incomprehensible how the Buddha could let man be preoccupied merely with his own redemption and not also with that of the Universe. Therefore it set up as an ideal that the man who has attained deliverance from reincarnation should renounce entrance into Nirvāna in order to appear again and again on earth and strive for the deliverance of all living creatures. On these saints who again and again voluntarily accept human existence, Mahāyāna-Buddhism confers the rank and dignity of Bodhisattvas, that is to say candidates for Buddhahood.

Mahāyāna-Buddhism is a logical development of the original Buddhism.

The Buddha ponders over the idea of compassion. But at the same time he makes man still in quite egoistic fashion think only of his own deliverance from the cycle of transmigration.

Mahāyāna-Buddhism takes account of the fact that the idea of compassion, once it is there, cannot be satisfied with just any kind of part allotted to it, but wants to dominate thought completely and must therefore demur to all egoistic longing for redemption.

With magnificent sincerity Mahāyāna-Buddhism resists the temptation to trace its origins to the Buddha by " cooking " tradition. It does not deny that the Buddha urged men before all things to strive after deliverance from reincarnation, and that he himself talked of entering into Nirvāṇa. But this he did only, the Mahāyāna teachers explain, because his contemporaries would not have been capable of understanding the higher truth that one ought to renounce Nirvāna. Therefore we must set the teaching that proceeds from the spirit of his compassion above that which was preached from his lips.

So, according to the Mahāyāna doctrine, Gotama Buddha did not enter into Nirvāna at all, but is labouring on and on in heavenly regions for the spreading in the world of the knowledge of redemption. " He pours down the great rain of religion and makes the big drum of religion thunder forth ".

Mahāyāna-Buddhism reached its full development in north-east India, probably during the two first centuries of our era. Its sacred writings are not, like those of the older Buddhism, in the Pāli language, but in Sanskrit.

Mahāyāna-Buddhism reached Tibet and China and was there preserved, whilst in India in the course of centuries Buddhism disappeared altogether; consequently we possess a series of important Mahāyāna texts, of which the Sanskrit originals have been lost, in Tibetan and Chinese translations.

The best-known work of Mahāyāna-Buddhism is the Saddharmapundarīka (the Lotus of Good Doctrine). It glorifies Gotama Buddha as a divine being enthroned on a mountain surrounded by thousands of gods and Buddhas and Bodhisattvas. This text was probably in existence before A.D. 200. As early as A.D. 223 and again in A.D. 286 it was translated into Chinese.

The Lalitavistara (" The Complete Story of the Play", to give it in full, " of the Buddha ") describes in legendary fashion how the divine Buddha took human form in the

Śākhya family and gives an account of his work on earth. The oldest portions of the text probably originated before the Christian era.

The Sukhāvatīvyūha ("A Complete Description of the Blessed Land") treats of Buddha Amitābha and the Sukhāvatī-Paradise. This work was translated into Chinese as early as between A.D. 147 and 186.

Nāgārjuna (2nd century A.D. ?), a member of a Brahmin family, and the learned poet Śāntideva (7th century A.D.) are great teachers of Mahāyāna.

* *
*

In Mahāyāna-Buddhism, then, the Buddha's idea of compassion reaches its full development. Its followers aim at attaining to the perfection of "the great compassion". How profound is the saying, "As long as living creatures suffer, there is no possibility of joy for those who are full of compassion!" For the first time in the thought of mankind, world-view is dominated by the idea of compassion.

But this mighty compassion could not develop and exercise its full influence in a natural way. Like the original Buddhism, Mahāyāna-Buddhism too is imprisoned in world and life negation. So that like the former it can really only give its approval to non-activity. Like the former too, it cannot attribute any real importance to the help which goes to alleviate material distress. And like the former again, the only effective act of compassion it can recognise is the diffusion of the knowledge that redemption will be won by denial of the will-to-live.

Mahāyāna-Buddhism is concerned for the deliverance of all living creatures. But it is no more able than the Sāmkhya system and the Buddha to explain how it is possible and ought to come about.

So Mahāyāna compassion has its hands bound in just the same way as were those of the Buddha himself. Fundamentally it is nothing other than the compassion in thought which the Buddha made a duty for his monks, only it is raised beyond all bounds. Therefore it cannot any longer remain contemplative as in the Buddha, but lives to the full in compassionate desires, often in very orgies of compassionate desires.

The Mahāyāna believer prays for all beings, that they may suffer no want, be spared pain and sickness, not be deserted and oppressed, may pass a happy life free from thought of sin, and that from lower forms of existence they may enter into the higher forms which lead to redemption. Long intercessory prayers of this sort are found in the Mahāyāna writings. Because women are reckoned among the lower beings, supplication is made for them that they may be born again as men. In these prayers there is remembrance also of those who dwell in hell in anguish and torment. The " great compassion " applies not only to the creatures that dwell on earth, but to all living things in all worlds.

From Mahāyāna Texts.[1]—" In all lands may all the sufferings of living beings come to an end."—" May all living beings in the ten regions of the universe who are weak, sick, reduced in circumstances and unprotected be freed from their trouble."—" May the beaten be freed from

[1] These quotations are from Professor Moriz Winternitz's *Der Mahāyāna-Buddhismus* (Siebert und Mohr, Tübingen, 1930), pp. 46-47, 53; 61.

blows, may those who are threatened with death be restored to life, and may those who are in tribulation become free from all fear."—" May those who suffer hunger and thirst receive food and drink in abundance."

" May the blind see, the deaf hear, the women with child give birth painlessly."—" May sounds of pain be nowhere heard in the world. And may no single living being experience what is disagreeable."—" May living creatures avoid the low way" (reincarnation).—" May all women constantly be born again as men, as brave heroes and wise scholars."—" May they see the Buddhas in the ten regions of the universe, sitting comfortably in the glorious trees of precious stones on thrones of beryl, and may they hear the sermons they preach."

" May the torment and anguish of those who dwell in hell come to an end."—" May the fear of being devoured by each other quit the animals; may the ghosts be happy."—" I exult over the liberation of living beings from the sufferings of the cycle of reincarnation "

But Mahāyāna compassion does not exhaust itself merely in abstract wishes, but is concerned also with deeds expressed in wishes. The simple natural act of compassion is not taken into account at all. In the Mahāyāna texts there is indeed much talk to the effect that the hungry should be fed, the thirsty given drink, the sick nursed. But one seeks in them in vain for commands actually to give loving aid to alleviate distress. Mahāyāna-Buddhism ultimately only takes into consideration theoretical acts which contribute towards real complete deliverance from suffering existence. The " great compassion " does not allow the Mahāyāna believer, as the Buddha did, to be satisfied with announcing the truth which brings deliverance. It compels him to be willing in thought to give up for the redemption of others the treasure of good works which he has gained, to take upon himself the sufferings of others, to enter in their stead into a lower form of existence and for them to endure the pains of hell. Instead of simply practising compassion, he is occupied with great deeds of heroic self-sacrifice which he wants to accomplish as a Bodhisattva.

From Mahāyāna Texts.[1]—" May I lead all living beings into the city of Nirvāṇa."—" May I, for the sake of the good I have accomplished, be a soother of all sufferings of all beings."—" All merit which I have achieved, I here without concern give up for the welfare of all beings."

" I strive not merely for my own redemption. I must lead all these living beings . . . out of the flood of transmigration. I must take upon myself the whole mass of the suffering of all beings. In so far as I can, I will taste to the full all sufferings in all evil forms of existence as they are arrived at in all parts of the Universe . . . I am determined to live in every single form of existence for countless millions of periods of the Universe. . . . It is indeed better that I alone suffer than that all living beings should reach the abodes of the evil forms of existence."

" The Bodhisattvas who realise the connection (between themselves and other beings) and have pleasure only in the mitigation of others' sufferings rush into hell like flamingoes into a lotus grove."

St Paul similarly in exaltation utters the words (Epistle to the Romans, ix. 3) : " I could wish that myself were accursed from Christ for my brethren, my kinsmen according to the flesh."

In Mahāyāna-Buddhism compassion makes its appearance in such strength that really it ought to revolt

[1] Quotations from Winternitz, *Der Mahāyāna-Buddhismus*, 1930, pp. 39, 53, 34-35, 59.

against world and life negation and lay claim to the right of helpful activity. But world and life negation stand firm as a rock for later Buddhism, which remains its thrall although it contains in itself even more living instincts to activity than are found in the Buddha himself.

It is because compassion is so strongly developed in Mahāyāna-Buddhism that we see with such perfect clearness how unnatural it becomes through world and life negation. With the Buddha compassion is still in some degree able to pretend it is contented with non-activity. But in Mahāyāna-Buddhism it can no longer do this, but must endeavour to surmount the difficulties of the problem of non-activity by an illusion of imaginary activity.

But how wonderful that there was once a time when there were in the world millions of people so entirely dominated by feelings of compassion!

*   *
   *

It is interesting that Mahāyāna-Buddhism undertakes to find a basis for compassion in knowledge. For this it goes back to the denial of the *ego* by the Buddha. If there be no *ego*, he argues, then there is no difference between one *ego* and another. So the foundations of compassion are really laid in the fact that the thinking man must confess to himself that he cannot really define the boundaries between his own *ego* and those of other beings. In the exercise of compassion this truth of there being no distinction between the I and the Thou (Parātmasamatā) is known through the feelings.

From Mahāyāna Texts.[1]—" From habit we connect the conception of the self with our own body, which nevertheless has no self. Why does not the idea of the self as referring to others similarly arise also from habit ? "—" No man exists whose suffering is really his own. Of whom then can it be said, that it is *his* suffering ? All sufferings without distinction are ownerless. Because they are sufferings, therefore we must keep them off. What sense has any limitation in this (that is to say that one keeps off only suffering that one regards as one's own) ? "—" If fear and pain are as much hated by my neighbour as by myself, what then distinguishes my self that I should protect it more than I protect him ? "

On the ground of identity of the I and the Thou, as it follows from the doctrine of the Brahman, the Upanishads explain all love as self-love. " In truth ", says Yājñavalkya to his wife Maitreyī, " the husband is not dear for the husband's sake, but the husband is dear for the sake of the Self ", and " Living beings are not dear for the sake of living beings but living beings are dear for the sake of the Self ".[2] That is to say, because the same Brahman dwells in others as in ourselves, that which seems to us to be love for others is merely self-love of the Brahman.

So because of the impossibility of distinguishing between the I and the Thou, it is determined in that Upanishad that all love to one's neighbour is only the profoundest self-love. Mahāyāna-Buddhism on the contrary proves from that same impossibility that there can be no self-love, but only love for one's

[1] Quotations from Winternitz, *Der Mahāyāna-Buddhismus*, pp. 58-60, 44.
[2] Bṛhad-Āraṇyaka-upanishad, 2. 4.

neighbour. These contrary assertions come to the same thing in the long run. By both of them ethics are reduced to nothing by the explanations given. True ethics presume the absolute difference of one's own *ego* and those of others and accentuate it. The difference, however, is not a plain matter of course but an enigma.

* *
*

But Mahāyāna-Buddhism does not merely make use of the Buddha's theory of knowledge to explain ethics: it also develops it further as such. Those who undertake to do this are probably Brahmanic thinkers. Otherwise we could not well understand how the Buddha's theory of knowledge is made of service to a belief which is the counterpart of the Brahmanic doctrine of Māyā.

In the opinion of the teachers of Mahāyāna the Buddha only conceded some kind of reality to the world of the senses because his pupils would not have been able to grasp the truth that it has none. As a matter of fact, they said, he assumed that the outer world exists only in our consciousness. That he who knows regards what he knows as something different from himself with an independent existence of its own rests on illusion (Māyā). The outer world is a vision of conceptions which we carry within ourselves. The conformity to law which we observe in it is due to the fact that every conception is the result of a previous conception. In meditation and ecstasy man is liberated from the delusion that the world of the senses is real.

As this teaching, in opposition to the view of the Buddha, holds the conscious *ego* to be a spiritual reality, other Mahāyāna teachers, among them the celebrated Nāgārjuna (2nd century A.D. ?), advance to the assertion that we can assume the existence neither of a material nor of a spiritual reality. They devise the phrase, " All is nothing ". According to them, there is neither Being nor non-Being, but merely Nothing which is neither Being nor non-Being. Not only is the outer world which man perceives an illusion, but so also is his belief that he exists and perceives it. This doctrine is called the doctrine of absolute emptiness (Śūnyatā). It gains a footing, and in Mahāyāna-Buddhism actually attains the importance of a dogma.

But what is compassion doing in an unreal world ? How can Mahāyāna-Buddhism combine its ethics with its nihilistic doctrine of existence ?

This is only possible on the hypothesis of twofold truth. For if our existence and the existence of the Universe are merely the visions of a dream, they nevertheless as such have for us a relative reality. We must behave in a way which corresponds to the imagined world and our supposed existence in it. As this world seems to us full of suffering, it is our duty to strive to bring the suffering in it to an end. Following the usual course of thought and imagination, man holds to this relative truth, and through a life passed in a compassionate disposition and through faith in the grace of the divine Buddha attains to celestial bliss. The delusion about duties (Kāryamoha) does not matter. It is not merely harmless, but also beneficent.

But in self-submergence man has insight into the highest truth of " emptiness " and through it wins real deliverance from the delusion of existence.

The Buddha—and in this is seen his greatness—avoids having anything to do with a doctrine of twofold truth. But as a matter of fact it is present with him though it is hidden. Without embarrassment he premises the Self for the purposes of ethics, the Self whose existence he denies in his theory of knowledge. In Mahāyāna-Buddhism what is hidden in the Buddha becomes manifest.

In this impracticable distinction between an ethical, relative truth and an absolute truth which stands above all ethics, late Buddhist thought admits that it cannot acquire ethics from knowledge of the Universe and cannot combine knowledge of the Universe with ethics.

* *
*

Ceylon, Burma and Siam remain faithful to the older Buddhism.

According to tradition, Buddhism came to Ceylon through Mahendra, the son (or brother) of the famous Buddhist King of North India, Aśoka (272-231 B.C.). The name Aśoka is an abbreviation of Aśoka-Vardhana, which means " Increaser of freedom from care ".

At the beginning of his reign Aśoka, like his father, was a protector of the Brahmins. He was probably converted to Buddhism out of repentance for the conquests he had made with fire and sword. His kingdom comprised not only the valleys of the Indus and Ganges, but also large territories lying to the south of these rivers. He declared himself the protector and promoter of Buddhism and sent out Buddhist missionaries in all directions.

VII. Later Buddhism in India

Siam received Buddhism from Cambodia, where it is supposed to have begun to be known in the year A.D. 422. It is said to have reached Burma before the 6th century A.D.

The older Buddhism only suffered alteration in Ceylon, Burma and Siam in so far as in these countries it conceded importance also to popular religion and worship.

To celebrate his jubilee in the year 1893, King Chulalongkorn of Siam published a complete edition of the sacred writings of the older Buddhism belonging to the Tripiṭaka (the Three Baskets).[1]

To-day the older Buddhism is found only in Ceylon and Further India. In India proper (Hindustan)—except in Nepal, on the southern slopes of the Himalayas—Buddhism has altogether disappeared. In Nepal, China, Tibet, Korea and Japan it is Mahāyāna-Buddhism and derivatives of it that are found.

How comes it that Buddhism has ceased to exist in its own home-land, Hindustan?

It was not exterminated by persecutions, but gradually lost its adherents because it could not sustain the competition against Brahmanic teaching with its freshly increasing strength, and Hinduism, which became more and more widespread.

Its decline began about A.D. 800. About A.D. 1600 Buddhism—except in Nepal—ceased to exist in India (Hindustan).

The Brahmanic system and Hinduism are superior to Buddhism by virtue of their mysticism. They stand for the elemental idea of the union of the human spirit with the Spirit of the Universe. Thus they

---

[1] On these writings, see p. 90.

possess something simple and living which is lacking in Buddhism.

The denial by Buddhism of the idea of a highest and purest Being and the idea of the soul involves it in complications. It loses its connection with natural imagining and thinking, and its relationship to the natural piety of the Indian.

Buddhism (in common with the Sāmkhya doctrine and Jainism) is only concerned with the idea of deliverance from reincarnation. But this can never attain the significance of a real world-view. It is too narrow for that. The idea on the other hand of the union of the human spirit with the Spirit of the Universe does comprise a world-view. World-view can in some fashion fit into the idea of deliverance from reincarnation, if men's minds are preoccupied with this. But the idea of liberation from reincarnation cannot become a world-view. This is the real ground of the inferiority of Buddhism as compared with the Brahmanic doctrine and Hinduism. Thought cannot desist from seeking a real world-view.

If Buddhism was able to maintain itself for so many centuries in face of Brahmanism and Hinduism, it was because it is the creation of a great mind and because its ethics are superior to theirs. But in measure as the Brahmanic teaching and Hinduism, stimulated by Buddhism, develop ethically—and this is especially the case with Hinduism—their superiority as compared with that faith makes itself felt.

Brahmanism and Hinduism have the further advantage that they are in natural association with the religion of the people. The original Buddhism declared its independence of that. It is true that later

Buddhism resumed relations with it, but it no longer had the same position in relation to it that had Brahmanism and Hinduism.

And it surely contributed also to the decline of Buddhism in India that it rejected the old sacred writings of the Veda, whilst the Brahmins appeal to them from time immemorial and Hinduism reverences them more and more. And this, in the Indian Middle Ages—which began about the same time as in Europe—when the witness of the past was increasingly valued, became fatal for Buddhism. As it is not rooted in popular religion, it cannot lay claim to the sacred writings for its own purposes. The fact that the Buddha was not a reformer, but a revolutionist, brings its own retribution.

Speaking generally, the decay of the influence of Buddhism in India is to be explained by its uncompromising attitude in the question whether the man who is living a married life cannot also have a share in redemption. The Brahmanic and Hindu systems made to world and life affirmation the great concession that they did not merely tolerate marriage, but recognised it as enjoined by the commands of natural law. They asserted that man can attain to a state of blessedness in the existence in which he fulfils the duties of the father of a household. There are even sayings of Brahmanic teachers which assert that it is necessary for his redemption that a man should pass through the stage of being the head of a family.

With the Buddha on the other hand redemption can only be won in an existence entirely consecrated to world and life negation. Owing to the contempt for married life which accompanied this theory, his doctrine was at variance with popular feeling, which by tradition regarded the institution of marriage as sacred. That is why as time went on his radical world and life negation was defeated by the moderate world and life negation of Brahmanism and Hinduism.

It was Islam that gave the death-blow to Indian Buddhism. Between the years 1175 and 1340 Mohammedan conquerors who came from Persia founded their dominion over the greater part of India. Because Buddhism was not backed up by the religion of the people, it could not offer so tough a resistance to the new faith as did the Brahmanic doctrine and Hinduism. In Java also and in Sumatra and other Indian islands it was Islam that supplanted Buddhism; Jainism too, owing to Islam, lost the position it had previously held.

But indeed no complete explanation can be given of how it came about that Buddhism ceased to exist in India, the land of its origin, where for centuries it had exercised such great power over men's minds. So many events in the domain of spiritual history are in the nature of an enigma.

But that Buddhism ceased to exist does not mean that the Buddha had no more significance for India. At the time when the people renounced his radical world and life negation, his ethical ideas had already become common property. His ethical influence continues down to the present day.

Even his radical world and life negation is still in operation. Gandhi's esteem for celibacy may be traced back to the Buddha.

*   *

*

CHAPTER VIII

BUDDHISM IN CHINA, TIBET AND MONGOLIA

ACCORDING to a tradition which arose at the end of the 2nd century A.D., the Emperor Ming Ti of China (Later Han Dynasty), by reason of a dream in the year A.D. 61, sent a mission to India to fetch to his own country Buddhist teachers, texts and objects used in worship. In reality, knowledge of Buddhism had already reached China before our own era began, by way of northern India and eastern Turkestan. So it was the later Buddhism of northern India, from which the Mahāyāna doctrine developed, which spread in China.

As early as the middle of the 3rd century A.D. Buddhism had followers all over China and was already beginning to exercise some influence. In time the Mahāyāna system supplanted the earlier form of later Buddhism.

Between the 4th and 11th centuries A.D. numerous Chinese adherents of Buddhism came as pilgrims to India in order to visit the spots where the Master had sojourned and to fetch sacred writings. They usually chose the difficult route which leads through the desert of Central Asia, through the Tarim-Becken (Eastern Turkestan) and over the Himalayas, and more rarely the sea route via Further India. We possess valuable accounts of such pilgrimages by Fah-Hien and Hsüan Tsang. Fah-Hien's journey lasted from A.D. 399 to 414, that of Hsüan Tsang from A.D. 629 to 645. The latter brought home 657 Buddhist texts.

The majority of the many translations of Buddhist works into Chinese date from the period before A.D. 1000.

The so-called " Sūtra of the 42 Sections ", certainly one of the most ancient writings of Chinese Buddhism, is traced back to the two Buddhist missionaries who are supposed to have come to China in the 1st century A.D. with the ambassadors of the Emperor Ming Ti. It offers a short compendium of the later Buddhist teaching put into the mouth of the Buddha. Ethical thoughts have made their way into the foreground. But the Mahāyāna dogma, that there is no reality at all, is also preached.

* * *

How was it that Buddhism, with its negation of the world and life, could exercise such a force of attraction on the Chinese who in their simple way are devoted to world and life affirmation?

It certainly and above all was the enthusiastic ethics of Mahāyāna that enlisted their sympathy. From the time of Confucius (Kung-Tse, 551–479 B.C.) and his successors downward they were accustomed to inquiry about ethical duties. In Mahāyāna-Buddhism they now found an ethic which did not dictate to them in dry commandments, like that of Confucius, but was founded on profound reflections about the nature of Being. The grandeur and inwardness of the ethic of compassion fascinated them.

Buddhism, further, met their religious needs, needs for which Taoism had but little to offer, whilst Confucianism completely ignored them.

The great teacher of Taoism was Lao-Tse (born about

550 B.C. or somewhat earlier), the author of the Tao-Te-King. The original meaning of the word Tao is path. In its metaphorical sense it signifies the fundamental principle of what happens in the Universe. The Tao-Te-King in a collection of aphorisms teaches life in harmony with this.

Along with Lao-Tse, Lieh-Tse (about 440–370 B.C.) and Chuang-Tse (about 380–310 B.C.) may also be named as well-known representatives of Taoism.

Taoism—as becomes specially clear from the writings of Lieh-Tse—is a mysticism, stretching far back into prehistoric times, of union with the Primal Force at work in the Universe, a mysticism which originated in magical ideas and ecstatic experiences. Thus it has the same origin and is at bottom of the same nature as the magic mysticism to which the Brahmanic mysticism goes back. Lao-Tse was not, as is so often assumed, the creator of Taoism, but found it already there. Like Lieh-Tse and Chuang-Tse he made it nobler and more profound by developing from it spiritual and ethical truths.

Alongside of the philosophical Taoism developed by these thinkers, the primitive-religious form persists. In this the idea of union with the Primal Force is overgrown with ideas of magic, and to this union is especially ascribed the important feature that by means of it magical power is won. So it comes about that by Taoism we have to understand a grand, mystical, philosophical system and at the same time a primitive religious mysticism in which magical practices play a great part.

China knows no other popular religion than the Taoist. That is why Mahāyāna-Buddhism, which teaches love to Buddha - Amitābha, redemption through his grace and re-birth to a life of bliss in his heavenly Paradise, finds so great a response.

Through Taoism China is in a sense prepared for Buddhism. The Buddhist exercises in self-submergence in order to reach ecstasy are nothing new to the Taoists. They follow similar practices themselves.

Through Taoism Chinese thought is also in a position to enter into friendly relations with the Buddhist world and life negation. Lao-Tse and Chuang-Tse teach that man attains to being in harmony with what happens in the Universe by abstaining from activity—even from activity that ranks as ethical. All action ensuing on human plans, according to them, implies a disturbance of the Universe, which goes on its course in obedience to a mysterious, meaningful, ordered system. So right conduct consists in kindly inactivity.[1]

Lao-Tse and Chuang-Tse, however, do not leave the firm ground of world and life affirmation. They believe all that happens in the Universe as it appears in the world of the senses to be something that is full of meaning. But their doctrine of kindly inactivity has indeed much in common with that of Buddhism, although it rests on quite different hypotheses.

Thus it becomes explicable how the Chinese mind could feel so strongly attracted to Buddhism as to lose its sense of the fundamental difference between the world and life affirmation with which it was familiar and the Buddhist world and life negation, and how it came to exchange its own world and life affirmation for world and life negation. How potent must have been the effects on the Chinese of the fascination of the foreign system of thought when they became enthusiasts for the ideal of monastic life, which was so alien to their natural feeling and their tradition!

During the centuries when such things were hap-

---

[1] On Chinese ethics, see also pp. 84-87.

pening in China, in Europe the young peoples of the Great Migration (Völkerwanderung) were being led by the world and life negation of Greco-Roman Christianity to doubt their natural world and life affirmation, and were beginning to set a high value on the monastic ideal of life.

The Chinese understood Buddhism, then, as a kind of Taoism. To express its concepts and ideas, they drew on the vocabulary of Taoism. And Taoism on its side adopted expressions and thoughts from Buddhism.

At the present day Taoism still contains Buddhist elements.

Taoism and Buddhism of the noblest kind are found side by side in the commandments of the Rules of the Order of Taoist monks in China.

From the Commandments for Monks of Present-day Monastic Taoism in China.[1]—1st commandment: " Thou shalt kill no living thing, neither damage its life ".—2nd commandment: " Thou shalt not eat the flesh and blood of any living thing ".—3rd commandment: " Thou shalt drink no strong drink ".—4th commandment: " Thou shalt not eat the five bitter herbs ".[2]—5th commandment: " Thou shalt not utter flattery nor speak with a double tongue, nor utter untruths ".—6th commandment: " Thou shalt not make malicious nor insulting speeches ".—7th commandment: " Thou shalt not accept baseless lies as founded on fact, nor unproved lies as things proved ".—8th commandment: " Thou shalt not let thine eyes rest secretly on women and girls, and so shalt thou avoid awakening even the slightest of unchaste thoughts ".—9th commandment: " Thou shalt not steal from nor rob any one ".—10th commandment: " Thou shalt not fraudu-

---

[1] H. Hackmann, *The 300 Monastic Commandments of Chinese Taoism*, 1931.
[2] This means certain plants of the Allium family (garlic).

lently overreach others even to the value of a copper coin ".
—11th commandment: " Thou shalt not make attempts against any kind of property belonging to others ".—12th commandment: " Thou shalt not unrighteously covet the possessions of others ".

14th commandment: " Thou shalt not be ungrateful for the kindness and affection of thy teachers ".—15th commandment: " Thou shalt not envy the noble nor be jealous of the good ".—18th commandment: " Thou shalt not deceive and hoodwink old people and children ".

115th commandment: " Thou shalt not repulse beggars nor treat them with contumely ".—145th commandment: " Thou shalt not boast of thy ability to cure others ".—218th commandment: " Thou shalt be careful first to save others, afterwards thyself ".

The well-known commandments of compassion for animals from the Kan-Ying-P'ien are also found in these monastic Rules.[1] 34th commandment: " Thou shalt not whip nor beat . . . domestic animals ".—35th commandment: " Thou shalt not with intention crush beneath thy feet insects and ants ".—36th commandment: " Thou shalt not take delight in fish-hooks or arrows in order to get amusement ".—37th commandment: " Thou shalt not climb trees to take nests and destroy the eggs ".—63rd commandment: " Thou shalt not catch birds or animals in snares and nets ".—64th commandment: " Thou shalt not alarm and scare away birds sitting on their nests ".—65th commandment: " Thou shalt not pick flowers nor pluck up grass without reason ".—66th commandment: " Thou shalt not cut down trees without reason ".—67th commandment: " Thou shalt not burn commons nor hill-side woods ".—68th commandment: " Thou shalt not dig out animals hibernating in the earth in the winter months ".—112th commandment: " Thou shalt not pour hot water on the ground for the purpose of destroying insects and ants ".

---

[1] For the Kan-Ying-P'ien, see pp. 84-87.

According to a belief already found in China in the 2nd century A.D., Lao-Tse—who, says an old tradition, wandered westward after writing down the Tao-Te-King and ended his days in a foreign land—went to India and appeared there as the Buddha. It is a fact that Lao-Tse, the Buddha and Confucius were contemporaries.

Buddhism, at all events to begin with, found most of its patrons and followers in the circles of Taoist philosophy and Taoist popular religion.

* * *

In Chinese as in Indian Buddhism whole series of schools and communities (Tsungs) were formed. The question of the reality and non-reality of material and spiritual Being was discussed in them in all its bearings.

But the chief difference between them is that in some of them Buddhism was principally the religion of faith in Buddha Amitābha and bliss in a " pure land ", that is to say, in the Sukhāvatī Paradise, whilst in the others was fostered rather the true Buddhist meditation. The founder of the great school of meditation, also called the School of Inwardness (Hsin-Tsung), was the great Indian teacher Bodhidharma, who came—by the sea route—to China somewhere about A.D. 525 and worked there up to his death (A.D. 535). Bodhidharma exhorted his pupils to practise self-submergence. Through this alone, not through letters and learning, was the knowledge of the unspeakable truth of Being and redemption from the illusion of Being to be won. Later on—towards the end of the 6th century A.D.—the Chinese Buddhism of meditation also constructed for itself a cult.

A lower form of Buddhism, which like the most primitive Taoism sought to satisfy the superstition and belief in magic of the people, also developed, especially after the 8th century A.D. It called itself " The School of Secrets " (Mi-Tsung).

About A.D. 1050 a Buddhist monk issued a work with the title *Support of Religion*, in which he developed the view of Chinese Buddhism that the Buddha, Lao-Tse and Confucius preached one and the same doctrine. In the period which followed, statues of Lao-Tse and Confucius were erected in Buddhist monasteries and chapels by the side of those of the Buddha. Lao-Tse was given the place on his left, which is regarded in China as the place of honour, and Confucius that on his right.

About the year A.D. 1000 the spiritual and mental development of Chinese Buddhism came to a standstill. It really possessed no creative force of its own, but lived by the stimulation it received from India. This is the only comprehensible way in which we can account for the absence of controversy between the ethical world and life affirmation of the Chinese mind and the ethical world and life negation of Buddhism.

* * *

Chinese Buddhism could not constantly enjoy peace. At times it had to undergo severe persecutions. It was Confucianism that waged war against the foreign faith.

Under the T'ang Dynasty the Confucian dignitaries Fu-Yi (A.D. 624), Yao-Ch'ung (A.D. 714) and Han-Yü (A.D. 819) brought bills of indictment against Buddhism before the Emperors. In the year A.D. 844, under the Emperor Wu-Tsung, the first harsh persecution aimed at all foreign religions broke out, and it meant the end of Manichæism and the religion of Zarathustra in China and dealt to Buddhism blows from which it never fully recovered. Fortunately Wu-Tsung's successor, Hsüan-Tsung, brought the persecution to an end.

In the following centuries the rulers sought to put a stop to the undue multiplication of Buddhist monasteries. The founding of monasteries and entrance to the monastic life were made dependent on the permission of the authorities. Monasteries were often broken up, their estates confiscated, their bronze statues melted down to mint coinage, and their monks and nuns forced to go back and earn their living in ordinary life. In the year 1019 the pious Emperor Chên-Tsung (998–1022) of the Sung Dynasty (960–1127) for a time granted full liberty to Buddhism and Taoism alike, and in that same year upwards of 230,000 men and 15,000 women entered Buddhist cloisters! Chên-Tsung's successors found themselves compelled to return to the former measures in order to prevent the life of the people being endangered by Buddhism.

The Emperor Hui-Tsung (1101–1125) of the Sung Dynasty forbade the erection of statues of Lao-Tse and Confucius beside those of the Buddha, but without great success.

These measures taken by the authorities against Buddhism stopped it from spreading among the upper classes, but could do little to weaken its prestige among the masses.

And from time to time also there were reigning princes who more or less favoured it. Among these were Genghiz-Khan (1162–1227), the Mongol conqueror of Peking, and his grandson Kublai-Khan (*d.* 1294), the first Mongol Emperor of China.

Under the Ming Dynasty (1368–1644) and the Ch'ing (Manchu) Dynasty (1644–1912) Confucianism gained the upper hand, whilst Buddhism lost its influence more and more.

The outward decline was accompanied by spiritual decay. It became more and more a religion of the people, addressing itself to the quite uneducated and hardly continuing to possess any spiritual or ethical interests.

In the last few decades attempts, originating in Japan, have been made to uplift and reform Chinese Buddhism. We cannot yet tell whether they will have any success.

* * *

Buddhism reached Tibet in the 7th century A.D. under King Srong-btsan-sgam-po, who had for wives a Chinese and a Nepalese princess. It was at their wish that he introduced it.

The priests of the new religion gradually succeeded in taking possession of the power. In the 11th century they made an end of the monarchy. Tibetan Buddhism developed into a strongly organised church exercising temporal sovereignty.

The man who deserves the credit for the exalted

position of Tibetan Buddhism is the monk Tsung-kha-pa (" the man from the vale of onions "), who at the beginning of the 15th century A.D. appeared in its fold as a reformer. He succeeded in introducing monastic celibacy and strove against superstition and magic.

At the head of Tsung-kha-pa's reformed Tibetan Buddhist church are two Grand Lamas (Lama means the chief), who are regarded as incarnations of the Buddha. One—who since 1575 bears the title Dalai Lama (the Lama like the ocean)—resides in Lhassa, the other, the Pantchen-Erdeni-Lama (that is to say, the Lama who is the jewel among scholars), in the Ta-shi-lhum-po Monastery. The first is reputed to be the incarnation of the divine Bodhisattva Avalokiteśvara, the other that of Buddha Amitābha. The Grand Lama at Lhassa rules on earth, the other is more occupied with spiritual things. The successors of these Grand Lamas are sought among the boys born at the hour of their death. The origin of this custom is the belief that the Buddha who dwelt in the deceased Grand Lama is born again in a human form immediately after his death.

The commandment not to kill living creatures is only followed by the Buddhists of Tibet in a quite superficial fashion. They think it sufficiently observed, if they abstain from forms of slaughter which involve the shedding of blood. So when they lust after the flesh of a domesticated animal, they hold its mouth and nose and subject it to a cruel death by suffocation.

From Tibet the Buddhism of the Lamas spread in the 13th century to Mongolia, at the time when the great Mongol rulers conquered Tibet. Under Kublai-Khan the conversion of the Mongols made great progress.

Lamaistic Buddhism maintains its independence in face of Chinese Buddhism. Since China at the end of the 17th century A.D. made Tibet its vassal, a representative of the Dalai Lama at Lhassa resides in Peking. He too is regarded as an incarnation of the Buddha. And it is the same with the highest dignitary of Mongol Lamaism, who is resident at Urga.

The magnificent temples at Jehol, the summer residence of the Chinese Emperors of the Manchu Dynasty, lying north of Peking the other side of the Great Wall, which were robbed of their treasures when the Chinese Empire came to an end, were built in the 18th century for Lama worship.

It was permissible for the Emperors of China to show disfavour to Chinese Buddhism. But in order not to endanger their dominion over Tibet and Mongolia they were obliged to maintain an attitude of good-will towards the religion of the Lamas in North China as well, where it had spread. Since 1911, the Dalai Lama at Lhassa has been dependent on England. The Pantchen Lama, who is faithful to China, left Tibet years ago to reside in that country. But he will not be able to live permanently outside Tibet.

*   *

*

CHAPTER IX

BUDDHISM IN JAPAN

CHINESE Mahāyāna-Buddhism reached Japan in the 6th century A.D. from Korea. It at once spread at the court and among the nobility.

At the beginning of the 9th century A.D. Buddhism and the national Shintō religion joined forces. The gods of the Shintō religion were recognised as appearances of the celestial Buddhas and Bodhisattvas. This fusion was the work of the Buddhist monk Kōbō (774–835).

The original Shintō religion was a form of polytheism in which ethics played hardly any part. The gods were personified forces of Nature, appealed to for their protection. The sun, conceived as feminine, was regarded as the chief divinity. It is probably incorrect to say that Shintōism was essentially the religion of ancestor-worship, as the modern Japanese would like to believe.

Shintō-Buddhism therefore, called Ryōbu-Shintō (two-sided Shintō), received from Buddhism religious and ethical ideas. In ethics, furthermore, it was strongly influenced by Confucianism.

Japanese Buddhism was at first only connected with the Buddhism of China through the Korean form, but very soon it entered into direct relations with, and was strongly influenced by, Chinese Buddhism. Japanese monks journeyed, as Kōbō had already done, to China for the purpose of study.

From the beginning of the 10th century onward intercourse with China was interrupted for some 250 years, as Japan, for political reasons, closed its doors against it. But even during this period Japanese monks occasionally went to China. Along with Buddhism, Confucianism also spread in Japan.

From the end of the 12th century, from the time when Japan resumed intercourse with China, a vigorous religious life made itself felt in Shintō-Buddhism. Movements were developed within it which corresponded to the great Chinese schools.

* * *

The Buddhism of Meditation of the "School of Inwardness", founded by Bodhidharma in the 6th century, was spread in Japan by Myōan Eisai (1141–1215), the founder of the Zen sect.[1] This sect counted its followers principally among the members . . . of the warrior caste.

There is a tradition that in order to be able to keep awake during the nocturnal exercises in meditation by drinking tea as did the Chinese disciples of Bodhidharma, the Zen Buddhists brought seeds of the tea-plant from China to Japan and introduced its cultivation. Tea-planting had already been tried in Japan at an earlier period, but had been given up.

The Jōdo sect (Sect of the Pure Country that is to say, of Paradise), which also sprang into being at the end of the 12th century A.D., stands for the Chinese

[1] For the Buddhism of Meditation of Bodhidharma, see p. 144.

Buddhist doctrine of redemption through the grace of Buddha Amitābha, who in Japan is called Amida-Butsu (Butsu is the Japanese name for the Buddha). Its founder was the monk Genkū (1133–1212), the spiritual adviser of three Japanese Emperors.

At the age of seventy-four, however, he was banished for three years to the island of Shikoku by the third of these Emperors, Go-Toba, because he had persuaded one of his favourite wives to become a nun.

The thoughts of Genkū were further developed by his pupil Shinran (1173–1262), the founder of the Jōdo-Shinshū sect, that is to say " the True Sect of the Pure Country ". Whilst Genkū taught that entry into Paradise follows on faith in the grace of the Amida-Buddha and good works, Shinran asserted that faith in the grace of the Amida-Buddha alone comes into consideration. Man is not in a position in any way to earn bliss by his own merits. In spite of this, Shinran required ethical conduct, and, be it noted, required it like Luther, as the expression and fruit of faith in redemption.

Like Luther, Shinran rejected pilgrimages, exercises in penance, fasting, superstition and all magical practices. He abolished the celibacy of the priesthood, of the monks and of the nuns. True piety was to be preserved in the family and in the worldly calling. He recommended to the laity the diligent study of the holy scriptures. And he demanded that the people should be delivered from their ignorance by good schools.

He did not admit that women are less capable than men of attaining to the state of bliss.

Like Luther he composed hymns intended for use at divine service in praise of the redemption which follows upon grace. In the conduct of worship he assigned an important place to the sermon.

The Jesuit missionaries who came to Japan in the middle of the 16th century at once became aware of the relationship between Jōdo-Shinshū-Buddhism and the " Lutheran Heresy ". Father Francesco Cabral reported on it in a letter dated 1571.

In Japan, then, there arose a Buddhism in which world and life affirmation took the place of world and life negation. There was no argument between the two ; the former with magnificent ingenuousness simply reinterpreted Buddhism in its own sense. So what the Chinese mind could not do, the Japanese mind accomplished. But the ethical world and life affirmation of Confucius, with which it had been familiar for centuries, came to its aid in this.

It was because of its ethics that Buddhism was able to enter into alliance with world and life affirmation.

Although Buddhism and Christianity have their roots in world and life negation, they nevertheless have affinity with world and life affirmation because their ethics of perfection of heart contain the principle of love and within that principle lies the impulse to activity. They can be lifted out of world and life negation and transplanted into world and life affirmation.[1]

Thus Japanese world and life affirmation transforms Buddhism and makes it harmonise with its own spirit. In similar fashion modern European world

[1] On this, see also pp. 113, 114.

and life affirmation gives a fresh interpretation, in its own sense, of the teaching of Jesus. In both cases violence is done to history, but violence which is justified, in so far as the Buddhist and Christian ethics of love, by their instinct to activity, strive to escape from world and life negation, and can only attain to full development in world and life affirmation.

How greatly a world and life affirming form of religion appeals to the Japanese nature is seen in the great response evoked by Jōdo-Shinshū-Buddhism. At the present day at least two-fifths of the population are followers of this faith.

* * *

Of course the doctrine of Shinran is an outrage on Buddhism The monk Nichiren (1222–1282) rebelled passionately against the betrayal of the original spirit of Buddhism. His self-adopted name means Sun-lotus. He condemned together the Zen sect, the Jōdo sect and the Jōdo-Shinshū sect. Faith in the saving grace of the Amida-Buddha he characterised as a damnable heresy. Redemption can only be won by the "path of holiness", that is to say, by renunciation of the world.

Nichiren believed he was sent by the Buddha to renew his true doctrine. And this indeed he did when he emphasised the value of world-renunciation and the monastic life. But his doctrine of Being is not that of the Buddha, for he thinks on pantheistic lines. All that is, according to him, participates in the essential nature of the Proto-Buddha. On this he based his hope of world-redemption, and from this standpoint he concluded that animals, plants, stones and all lifeless objects are called to the attainment of the glory of Buddha.

It was because Nichiren appeared not only as the accuser of rationalistic world and life affirming Buddhism, but also of the government which tolerated it, that he suffered persecution and for many years banishment. He was even condemned to death, but was reprieved at the last moment when he had already knelt down to suffer decapitation.

His doctrine, which was of a nature to gain the sympathy of primitive religious feeling, spread especially among the common people.

The Catholic Christianity which the famous Jesuit missionary Francis Xavier began to preach in Japan in the year 1549 had remarkable success there at first. A great outlook opened before it when after thirty years the Vice-Regent of the Empire, Nobunaga, who would have liked to break the political power of the Buddhist priesthood, showed it favour. But after his murder in the year 1582 it was completely exterminated in cruel persecutions.

From the 17th century onward we see the gradual rise of a national movement aiming at the restoration of the imperial power, which had been encroached upon by the nobility, and at the same time at that of the pure Shintō religion. By a series of imperial edicts issued between 1868 and 1873, the connection between Shintōism and Buddhism which had endured for centuries was ended and Shintōism was proclaimed the State religion. Buddhism lost its share in the temples and their estates. But in the year 1884 Shintōism again ceased to be the national religion; in 1889 full religious freedom was granted. So

Japanese Buddhism, which had adapted itself to the Japanese nature by its world and life affirming ethics and had achieved so much of importance in its social activities, was able again to develop side by side with Shintōism without let or hindrance.

There is scarcely any conflict between the two. Modern official Shintōism really has not the significance of a religion. It makes it the duty of all who belong to this people to venerate their ancestors, the Emperor and the Nation. But this can be reconciled with their adherence to another religion which is capable of satisfying their personal needs

The original Shintō religion must be distinguished from modern official Shintoism. Countless Japanese, especially country people, live in the faith to-day just as they did centuries ago. Many of them at the same time profess Buddhism.

In the last few years Japan has begun to work very energetically for the propagation of Buddhism in the world. The recently founded International Buddhist Society has its headquarters in Tokio. This Society is aiming at founding a Universal Buddhism based on the Ancient Buddhism of India.

But it is impossible to conceive how it will manage to reconcile Ancient Buddhism and Later Buddhism, and in particular the world and life negation of Indian Buddhism, with the world and life affirmation of Japanese Buddhism.

* *
*

CHAPTER X

THE LATER BRAHMANIC DOCTRINE

LET us return to the India of antiquity.
In the course of the debate they carried on for centuries with the Sāṃkhya doctrine, Jainism and Buddhism, the Brahmins felt the need of clearly defining in its main outlines the doctrine, incoherently taught in the Upanishads, of identity with the Universal Soul. They called it the Vedānta doctrine, that is to say, the teaching which is contained at the end (Anta means end) of the Veda, which the whole Veda has in view. For they regard the Upanishads as the conclusion and crown of the Veda.

The Vedānta doctrine was finally fixed in the Brahmasūtras of Bādarāyana, the head of a school probably at some time during the fourth century of the Christian era.

Sūtra means " thread ", in its figurative sense " short rule ". It is a metaphor taken from weaving. The Brahmasūtras are in a certain sense the threads stretched out as warp, from which, through the oral explanation added as woof, there comes into being the complete fabric of the doctrine. These short sentences intended for committing to memory are by themselves often incomprehensible in their brevity.

In the 555 Sūtras of Bādarāyana the teaching of the Upanishads is expressed with a view to refuting the beliefs of the Sāmkhya doctrine (in so far as they have not been adopted by Brahmanism), of Jainism and of Buddhism.

Of course the Brahmasūtras cannot give to the teaching of the Upanishads any real coherence, but only an appearance of consistency. They cannot succeed in the impossible task of really reconciling the mysticism of identity with the Soul of the Universe and the doctrine of reincarnation and deliverance from it.[1]

Nor do the Brahmasūtras make any attempt to go to the root of the problems contained in the Upanishads. They only endeavour, not without skill, to find serviceable decisions on the path of compromise. They are the starting-point of Brahmanic scholasticism.

It is remarkable that they reject the doctrine of Māyā. They do ascribe some kind of reality to the world of the senses, and in this way are the representatives of the original Brahmin teaching. But to the question, why the Brahman makes individual souls and a world of the senses proceed from itself, they too know no better answer than that it is a play. So it is impossible for them to attribute real importance to ethics.

They emphasise strongly that redemption may be attained by no kind of works, but through knowledge alone. They deal exhaustively with the exercises for arriving at self-submergence. The ancient Brahmanic belief that knowledge of identity with the Brahman must be experienced in ecstasy is to them a matter of course.

[1] On this question, see pp. 48-55.

All later expositions of the Brahmanic doctrine take the form of commentaries on the Brahmasūtras. This shows that Brahmanism henceforth follows the ways of scholasticism.

* * *

The greatest of the commentators is Saṃkara (9th century A.D.), born of a Southern Indian Brahmin family to be the Thomas Aquinas of Brahmanism.

Saṃkara does not cling to the belief of the Brahmasūtras, but interpolates his own belief even when it is quite different. He recognises that the doctrine of Māyā is a logical conclusion from the Brahmanic view of Being. Like the representatives of Later Buddhism, therefore, he assumes that the world of the senses exists only in our imagination. But as something persistently imagined it has, he explains, practical reality.

Saṃkara's strict monism is called the doctrine of Non-duality (Advaita) because he admits no other reality beside the Brahman. He has the later Upanishads on his side.[1]

As in Later Buddhism, so too in Śaṃkara's teaching a lower exoteric truth exists beside the higher and esoteric. The highest truth for him is that man, through knowledge of the identity of his own self with the Brahman, should experience his unity with the Brahman and his freedom from the world of the senses already in this life. The lower truth consists in a doctrine of redemption focussed on the doctrine of reincarnation. According to this, even those who are

[1] On this, see pp. 59, 60.

not capable of true knowledge of the Brahman nevertheless participate in union.

Man is the slave of the lower truth, if he attributes reality to the world of the senses and fails to perceive the true nature of the Brahman, but believing it to be the highest divine personality, worships it as such and longs for a state of bliss in the Brahman-heaven. Śaṃkara derives the right to ascribe the importance of truth to what he must have regarded as error from the fact that these phantoms of the imagination are the effect of the Brahman, that they have practical reality for man because he constantly lives among them and that even the Upanishads concede their validity. That the Upanishads speak of the Brahman as the Absolute without qualities and also as the highest God, he explains—of course wrongly—by saying that they distinguish between a higher and a lower Brahman. The real explanation is that in many passages of the Upanishads the Brahman wears the features of a Brahmanic divinity.[1]

In order, then, to establish his doctrine of twofold truth on the foundation of the sacred writings—which as a scholastic he feels to be his duty—Śaṃkara makes the bold assertion that even in the Upanishads a higher and a lower truth are found side by side.

The Brahman-divinity according to him is in a sense the first production of the magic play which the Universal Soul stages for itself. Then the Brahman-divinity produces the Universe. Thus Śaṃkara advances to meet the popular religion and concedes to theism also the right of existence.

In many respects his doctrine of the higher and

[1] On this, see pp. 56-58.

the lower Brahman is analogous to the hypothesis in Greco-oriental Gnosticism of a highest God and a demiourgos (creator of the Universe) who has proceeded from him and is inferior to him.

Those, then, who regard the world of the senses as real, and believe the Brahman to be a divinity according to the lower truth, through right worship of this Brahman-divinity can attain to this—that after their death they will not be born again " but will enter into the lower Brahman ", that is to say, will lead a blissful existence in the company of the Brahman-divinity.

From this lower state of bliss they then at some later period without further ado attain to the state of real absorption in the pure Brahman. For at the end of every period of the Universe the Brahman-divinity, along with the Universe that proceeded from him, returns into the Universal Soul. The souls that have entered into his state of bliss participate in this return. In this way they are reunited to the Universal Soul. Never again do they enter earthly existence, not even in future periods of the Universe.

Thus the hypothesis of successive periods of the Universe derived from the Sāṃkhya doctrine enables Śaṃkara to change the provisional bliss of deliverance from reincarnation during the current period of the Universe into the permanent bliss of union with the Brahman. His views, too, on matter, the individual soul and its relations with the body, contain much that belongs to Sāṃkhya. Of course, even Śaṃkara does not succeed in combining in a really satisfactory way the conceptions of the Sāṃkhya teaching and the idea of the mysticism of identity with the Brahman. He does not even attempt it.

St Paul also distinguishes a provisional and a positive state of bliss. The provisional state consists in participation in the Messianic Kingdom, which is imagined as limited by time. According to the Apocalypse of John (ch. xx. 7) it lasts a thousand years. It begins with the Parousia, that is to say, with the return of Jesus in His Messianic glory. Those alone have a share in this Kingdom who belong to the last generation living on the earth, who heard the Gospel from Jesus and as a result believed in Him as the Messiah. If they are already dead when the end of the world begins, they experience a special resurrection before the other dead, the so-called resurrection of the just; if they are still alive, they will be transformed into supernatural beings. They triumph with the Messiah over the powers hostile to God who ruled the world. The last of these enemies to be overcome will be death. Immediately after, the resurrection of all men and women who have ever dwelt on earth takes place, and with this begins the Kingdom of eternal bliss which replaces the Messianic Kingdom. In the Kingdom of eternity it is no longer the Messiah, but God, who reigns. He is now again " All in All ". Those who participate in the Messianic Kingdom all go on without further ado to eternal bliss. Judgment is held over those who only rose from the dead at the dawn of the Kingdom of eternity. Some gain eternal joy, others are condemned to eternal death. (First Epistle to the Corinthians, ch. xv. 23–28.)

Taking into account that the Brahmanic doctrine of Being, if it be logically thought to a conclusion, must maintain the non-reality of the world of the senses, Śaṃkara resolved to adopt the hypothesis of a twofold truth. He was driven to it in the same way as the teachers of Later Buddhism, who as the result of their views on Being similarly arrived at the assertion that the world of the senses is not real.

At the same time Śamkara has a perception of

the fact that the mysticism of union with the Brahman and the doctrine of redemption which accompanies the doctrine of reincarnation are two quite different things. The hypothesis of a twofold truth makes it possible for him to keep them apart. So he preaches the mysticism of union with the Brahman as the higher truth in conformity with the fact of the non-reality of the world of the senses. Alongside this, as a lower truth, he allows currency to a doctrine of redemption from reincarnation which assumes the reality of that world of the senses. In an external fashion he connects them with each other by making the soul redeemed from reincarnation return for ever into the Brahman at the end of the world period.

But why does he abandon the axiom, hitherto championed by the Brahmins and still strictly guarded in the Brahmasūtras, that deliverance from reincarnation and union with the Brahman can be attained through nothing save only through perfect knowledge? Why does he make to popular religion the concession, which is really impossible from the Brahmanic standpoint, that this may also be arrived at by pious worship of the Brahman imagined as God?

He is forced to this because in the course of time there had arisen a higher popular religion of a monotheistic nature which had gained so high a repute that account had to be taken of its doctrine of redemption. This religion of the people is monotheistic Hinduism.

Hinduism teaches that by profound self-devotion to God deliverance from reincarnation and absorption into God can be attained. The Brahmins could no longer ignore this living mysticism of love to God since with time it had become so widely disseminated.

They were obliged either to take up a position against it or assign it a place in their doctrine. The latter alternative was the only one that they could consider. So now they themselves teach the worship of the Brahman in the guise of God as mysticism of a second order.

The Later Buddhist doctrine of redemption through faith in the divine Buddha-Amithāba also arose under the influence of monotheistic Hinduism.[1] It is the counterpart of the exoteric redemption doctrine of Later Brahmanism. Śamkara is not the originator of this doctrine. He found it present in the Brahmanism of his time and legitimised it. But the Brahmasūtras make no mention of it, but keep strictly to the Upanishads.

Samkara is called the completer of the Brahmanic doctrine. He is that, but at the same time he is the beginning of its end. He thinks out in detail the Brahmanic mysticism of union with the Universal Soul, and preserves for it its majestic greatness. But at the same time he admits another mysticism to a place beside it. He is like the Roman Emperors who planted colonies of foreign peoples within their Empire and thought in this way to make an end of the danger to it which they threatened.

The Hindu mysticism of self-devotion to God is superior to the Brahmanic in its vitality and also because it is capable of assuming an ethical character. That is why it could not always remain in the subordinate position assigned to it by Śaṃkara. Its practical superiority was bound sooner or later to end in its taking the place of Brahmanic mysticism and only allowing it a nominal continuance.

[1] For this doctrine, see pp. 121, 122; 144; 151-154.

Śamkara made concessions only to the other form of mysticism, not to ethics as well. He vigorously opposed the opinion that redemption from re-birth is dependent not alone on higher or lower knowledge but also on ethical behaviour. How near he might have been to demanding further from the second way of redemption, not only worship of the Brahman-divinity, but also self-devotion to that divinity in ethical activity! But this seemed to him irreconcilable with Brahmanic thinking. He seemed to apprehend the lower Brahman as a personality, but not as an ethical personality. He definitely remarks that for the Brahman, for the lower as for the higher, there is neither good nor evil.

So Śamkara remains true to the old doctrine that ethical conduct is only an aid to a better reincarnation but does not effect redemption. And he recognises no validity for any other motive for morality except the egoistic. He considers only what a man attains by it for the improvement of his reincarnation, not what is achieved and accomplished by it. It is as if he had a presentiment of the danger which threatens Brahmanic mysticism through ethics. Therefore he makes a point of strongly emphasising that ethics belong only to the exoteric truth and, moreover, only occupy a subordinate position in that. For any believer in the Māyā doctrine ethics can have only a quite relative importance.

Śamkara's recognition of a way of redemption which even people who remain in ordinary life may tread means a tremendous concession by Brahmanic world and life negation to world and life affirmation. But he does not discuss the matter.

CHAPTER XI

BRAHMANIC WORLD-VIEW IN
THE LAWS OF MANU

IN the famous ancient Book of the Laws of Manu (Manu-Smṛti) we find Brahmanic world-view applied to ordinary life.

Manu is the divine Primeval Father of the human race. The Brahmin-divinity is said to have revealed to him the laws valid for individuals and for society, and his son Bhṛgu communicated them to human beings.

Manu's Law Book originated somewhere between 200 B.C. and 200 A.D. But it certainly contains matter that belongs to a much earlier period.

The six first sections of the work treat of the creation of the world and the order of Brahmins, the seventh of the king and his duties, the eighth and ninth of the laws, the tenth of castes and semi-castes, the eleventh of acts of atonement, the twelfth of reincarnation and redemption.

According to this book the Brahmins are appointed by the Brahman-divinity lords over all that the world contains. They are to be venerated as god-like beings. A Brahmin at ten years old must be as much respected as if he were the father of a hundred-year-old member of the warrior class. And even if a Brahmin has committed every kind of crime, he may not be condemned to death, but only to banishment. The worst sin that a man can load upon himself is the murder of a Brahmin. He must expiate it with death and will be born again as a savage beast. Anyone who seizes a Brahmin by the hair is to have his hands cut off; anyone who steals a cow from a Brahmin shall have one foot mutilated.

If a man dies without leaving natural heirs, his property shall go to the Brahmins.

If a Brahmin finds buried treasure, it belongs to him in its entirety; if the King finds such, he must share it with the Brahmins. By his deferential behaviour to a Brahmin, a member of a lower caste can attain to reincarnation in a higher.

But at the same time the Laws of Manu show the Brahmins their duties. They say the ignorant Brahmin is a useless creature, and compare him with an elephant carved out of wood.

The Brahmin must be without avarice, without arrogance, without guile, hospitable and kind. In every respect he must endeavour to walk blamelessly. Even to the members of the lowest caste he is to be friendly in demeanour.

He is forbidden to tell fortunes, to practise magic, to study astrology.

He must observe in the strictest manner the commandment not to kill and not to hurt (Ahiṃsā). But he is allowed to slaughter in sacrifice and to eat the meat of the victim.

The first quarter of his life is to be passed under his parents' roof and with his teacher; the second as the head of his family; at the beginning of the third quarter, when his sons have issue, he is to withdraw into the forest as a hermit; in the course of the fourth he is to loosen the last bonds that still unite him to earth in order that he may concentrate his mind as an ascetic entirely on union with the Brahman.

In a holy attitude of mind he is to guard the freedom from the world he has gained. His words are to be purified in truth; his heart is to be pure. He must endure insults, disdain no one, bear enmity to none. Nor must he requite anger with anger. He is to reply to insult with good words.

It is doubtless due to Buddhist influences that Manu's Law Book replaces the ancient Brahmanic supra-ethical world and life negation—of which it still makes mention—by ethical world and life negation.[1]

The Brahmin ascetic is not to seek death, but is to wait for it as a servant awaits his wages.

* * *

The King also is to be venerated as a divinity in human form. The maintenance of the law and the protection of the weak against the strong are his duty.

" If the King did not untiringly mete out punishment, the stronger would roast the weaker like fish on a spit; the crow would devour the sacrificial cakes; the dog would lick the juices of the sacrifice; property would no longer be stable, and everything would be topsy-turvy."

" The whole world is kept in order by punishment; a man who is virtuous (by nature) is hard to find."

But only the punishment inflicted by a virtuous king has the right effect. " Only if the King endeavours to govern his own desires is he able to keep

---

[1] Concerning these two varieties of world and life negation, see pp. 76-78.

his subjects in obedience." He must avoid hunting, playing with dice, sleeping during the day, backbiting, women, drink, dancing, music and unnecessary travelling.

He must learn a modest demeanour from the old Brahmins.

He shall abstain from violence and not unjustly arrogate to himself what belongs to his subjects.

In battle he shall bear himself as a knight. He must not strike down the opponent who is disarmed, who has taken to flight, or who is ready to surrender himself a prisoner. He must use neither poisoned arrows nor treacherous cunning.

He shall show mildness towards his subjects. If he must punish, let it be first with simple words, then with severe blame, then by a fine, and only when everything else fails by corporal punishment.

"As the leech, the calf and the bee drink in small draughts, so shall the King raise the yearly taxes with mature deliberation and only by degrees."

He must be a mild master also to those of low degree. If he is insulted by people who are suffering misfortune, he shall pardon them. "As the earth maintains all creatures, so shall the King maintain his subjects." He must always be mindful to protect the weak, the widows and childless women, and to care for all who are in distress.

In the conduct of external affairs he shall seek counsel from experienced Brahmins. He shall try to effect his conquests by fair means. He may practise bribery in the interest of the State. It belongs to his duty to mistrust his enemies and sow dissension among them. But above all his endeavour must ever be directed to winning them over by well-conducted negotiations.

He must see to it that his city is properly fortified.

* * *

The laws deal with the right judicial procedure, with borrowing, contracts, buying and selling, defamation, theft, bodily injury, marriage, repudiation of wives, adultery, rights of inheritance, liability to arrest, caste duties and the observance of caste distinctions.

Theft is severely punished. For the theft of jewels and kidnapping the penalty is death. Members of the lower castes incur milder punishment than those of the higher.

"Gambling and betting are to be treated as theft and shall not be tolerated by the King." He is to employ corporal punishment against these "masquerading thieves".

Theft must not be punished by death unless the stolen property is found with the thief, when there can be no doubt of his guilt.

Violence is regarded as a still more serious crime than theft.

The man who exercises his right of corporal chastisement on his wife, his children, his slaves and his pupils may strike them only on the back, not on the head.

The man who cannot pay a debt must work it off as the slave of his creditor.

A sale agreed upon may be annulled by either party within ten days.

A girl who has reached a marriageable age must wait three years to see if she is desired in marriage. When this time has elapsed, she is allowed, within the limits of her caste, to seek a husband for herself.

"Conjugal fidelity shall endure until death. This is to be regarded as the highest law for man and wife." Adultery is punishable, according to the circumstances, by fine, corporal chastisement or death. It is considered an aggravating circumstance, if the guilty have in addition disregarded the distinctions of caste.

The Laws of Manu speak disparagingly of women, but nevertheless guard their rights. Only when a wife has remained unfruitful for seven years may the husband repudiate her. If all the children she has borne die, he may do this after nine years. He is only allowed to divorce himself from a good and virtuous but constantly ailing wife with her permission.

A woman with child, like the Brahmin and the ascetic, has the right to use the ferry over a river free of charge.

As a principle the Laws of Manu are opposed to the remarriage of widows. But they tolerate it as an existing custom.

There is not a word in the Laws of Manu about the burning of widows. It is first mentioned in the later law books. And yet the custom must be an ancient one, as it was known to the Greek authors of the time of Alexander the Great. Originally it was probably confined to the ruling families and the warrior caste and even here was not the rule. It was never in general practice. In the year 1829 it was forbidden by the English authorities.

The Cāṇḍālas must dwell outside the villages.

They are only allowed to own dogs and donkeys and broken crockery.

The enjoyment of intoxicating beverages is forbidden to members of the three highest castes. Brahmins and members of the warrior caste shall not lend money at interest.

Need and famine abrogate all the commandments which concern the distinctions of caste. If he can get nothing else to eat, it is even permissible for the member of a higher caste to eat dog's flesh handed to him by a Cāndāla.

The observance of the commandment not to kill and not to hurt—except in the case of sacrifice—is inculcated in the most stringent terms. Manu's Law Book even endeavours to adopt the Jaina condemnation of agriculture. It quotes as the opinion " of virtuous people " that tilling the soil can be no praiseworthy occupation, because the earth and the little creatures that live in it are damaged. But at the same time it admits that others even regard it as good.

For the annihilation of a thousand little vertebrates a Brahmin has to make the same expiation as for the murder of a member of the lowest caste. If he has cut down fruit-trees, bushes, creepers or flowers, he must repeat a certain text from the Veda a hundred times.

In general : recitation of the Veda, sacrifice and asceticism wipe out guilt. Confession of the sin is also valued. " If a man who has committed a sin confesses it voluntarily, he is freed from it as a snake sloughs off its skin."

It is asceticism that has the highest expiatory effect. By it, if it be strictly followed, even the greatest crimes may be atoned. " Even insects, serpents, butterflies, birds and plants win heaven by the virtue of asceticism." So the problem of world-redemption is not foreign to the Laws of Manu.

Knowledge of the Vedas, asceticism, control of the passions, observance of the commandment not to kill and not to damage, fulfilment of the caste-duty, purity and practice of self-submergence—all these have to do with liberation from reincarnation.

In *Antichrist* (section 56) Friedrich Nietzsche calls Manu's Law Book " a work which is spiritual and superior beyond comparison, which even only to name in one breath with the Bible would be a sin against the Holy Spirit ". He bases this verdict on the fact that with this book the upper classes, the philosophers and warriors, hold the masses in their grasp. Therefore he finds in it an " affirmation of life ". " The sun shines over the whole book ", he writes.

He does not seem to have penetrated very deep into its spirit, or he would have noticed that it is full of life negation and that in it, as in the Old Testament law, a humanitarian attitude is just coming into being. Although it allows the caste distinctions to continue, Manu's Law Book takes up the cause of the weak against the strong and commands the strong to serve. So it has no more claim to Nietzsche's esteem than has the Bible.

In his *Will to Power* (sections 142 and 143) Nietzsche finds in the Laws of Manu " Semitism, that is to say, the spirit of priesthood, worse than anywhere ". He has no comprehension of the greatness and profundity of this spirit of priesthood.

*   *

*

CHAPTER XII

HINDUISM AND BHAKTI MYSTICISM

HOW did the Hindu thought arise to which the later Buddhism and the later Brahmanism had to make concessions in their doctrine?

About the year 1000 B.C. Indian polytheism, as we can see in the later Vedic hymns, was already in movement towards ethical monotheism. But the Brahmins took no part in this evolution which was going on. They had no interest in the improvement of the popular religion, because in reflection over the Brahman they had found quite a different starting-point for the path to higher knowledge.[1]

But the forces in the popular religion which were driving thought in the direction of ethical monotheism remained alive. The Brahmins' omission to further the development in progress certainly retarded, but did not end, it. Outside Brahmanism there arose prophetic personalities who assisted the ethico-monotheistic religion of the people to burst into flower.

We have no exact record of the course of this higher development, because for that older period we are entirely dependent on what the Brahmins thought good to hand down. We only know this much—that monotheism probably appears for the first time among the worshippers of the god Krishna.

[1] On this, see pp. 27-29.

The Origins of Monotheistic Hinduism

The rise of Krishna-worship again is wrapped in obscurity. Krishna (that is to say, the Black One), the son of Vasudeva and Devakī, is probably a deified tribal hero, later held to be an avatar of the god Vishnu. In the Vedic hymns Vishnu is not in the first rank of the gods. But as time goes on his prestige increases, until at last, though probably in circles outside of Brahmanism, he is reverenced as the one and only God.

But this popular religion which professes a belief in monotheism preserves polytheism beside it. It conceives the other divinities as appearances (Avatāras) of the only God. According to this religion, God is worshipped in the gods. So we find even in a hymn of the Rig-Veda : " They speak of Indra, Mitra, Varuna, Agni. . . . Although it is only one Being, the singers give it many a name."

In many Hindu religious communities the god Śiva occupies the place of Vishṇu. In others the Brahman-divinity is the Universal God.[1]

Hinduism is no coherent unity. It comprehends within it many forms of worship, not alone such as are of Aryan, but also such as are of primeval Indian, origin, and not only such as already show a monotheistic orientation, but also such as are still thoroughly fixed in polytneism.

Probably Krishna, the black god, was originally a primeval Dravidian divinity. This was certainly the case with Śiva and the goddess Kālī, *i.e.* the Black One, who plays so great a part in Hinduism.

When Hinduism is mentioned in the following pages, it is only the more highly developed popular religion that is meant, for which Krishṇa, Vishṇu, Śiva, Rāma, the

---

[1] For the Brahman-divinity, see pp. 30; 56-58; 159-161.

Brahman-god and other highest divinities are only manifestations of the one and only God.

For this form of Hinduism, Vishnu, Śiva and the deified Brahman provide a kind of trinity (Trimūrti). The same God has three names corresponding to the three forms of his manifestation and activity.

God is usually described in Hinduism as Bhagavat, that is to say, the Exalted.

*   *
 *

The monotheistic popular religion which comes into being alongside the Brahmanic faith does not adopt an attitude of opposition to it, for it regards Vedic lore as sacred and does not question the authority of the Brahmin priesthood.

And further: this popular religion is under the influence of Brahmanic thought, and that is why it develops in the direction of monotheism.

Hindu monotheism is distinguished from that of Zarathustra and from that of the Hebrew prophets in two respects. It sees God not as the Creator of the Universe existing beside and above the Universe, but as the Primal Cause from which the Universe has proceeded. And secondly, it does not simply demand of mankind obedience to God, but union with Him in complete self-surrender (Bhakti). So it is of a mystical nature, and in this we see that it has developed under the influence of the Brahmanic mode of thought. The mystical doctrine of Hinduism is related to that of Brahmanism like a moon to the sun from which it draws its brightness.

Bhakti piety takes its rise from the religion of the

aboriginal population. The conception of humble self-surrender to God is alien to the Aryans of India. But under the influence of Brahmanic mysticism the popular piety, originating from prehistoric times, of self-surrender to God assumed a mystical character.

Thus Hinduism is a popular religion which has become monotheistic and mystical under the influence of Brahmanic mysticism.

Many scholars have expressed the opinion, for which there are good grounds, that the Bhakti form of piety within Hinduism had its home in Southern India and spread thence to the north.

It must be noted that Śamkara, the Brahmanic teacher who first recognised the right of existence side by side with Brahmanic mysticism of the doctrine of redemption taught by the Bhakti form of religion, came from the south.[1]

Hindu mysticism is of a different nature from Brahmanic mysticism in so far as it is concerned with the uniting of the human personality to the divine Personality, not with the absorption of the individual soul into the Universal Soul. Hinduism does not lose itself in abstract thought, but strives to remain a living piety. It describes the right relationship of man to God as love (Bhakti), and it regards all the reverence which is shown to God in acts of worship as of secondary value compared with the striving for ever more complete self-surrender to Him.

In many Hindu hymns man's love of God is glorified under the metaphor of human love, just as the Christian mystics interpreted the Song of Solomon which concerns earthly love to express the longing of the soul for its Redeemer.

[1] For Śaṃkara and his doctrine, see pp. 159-165.

A further difference distinguishing Hindu mysticism from Brahmanic—and also from Christian—is that the ideal of quietism lies far from it. It does not urge man to leave ordinary existence, but expects him so to pass his life that in all things, in thought as in deed, he maintains his devotion to God.

Although it demands active self-devotion to God, nevertheless Hinduism professes a belief in world and life denial. It is so much under the influence of Brahmanic thought that it abandons the world and life affirmation which originally belonged to the religion of the people. So it dares not stand for the view that the universe in some way has a meaning and that human activity can set itself a task in the world. It nowhere makes the demand, which is such a matter of course to Christianity, that love to God shall be actively realised in love to man. Like the Brahmins it requires no other activity beyond what is imposed by the obligations of caste.[1]

It is also because it is so dependent on Brahmanic thought, that the older Hinduism only arrives at monotheism, and not at ethical monotheism. It regards God as a value completely exalted over the ethical and the non-ethical.

* * *

Thus Hinduism, along with all its subjection to Brahmanic world and life negation, preserves its independence only in one respect: instead of merely tolerating activity, it prizes it as a valuable thing.

---

[1] For the significance of activity required by the duty of caste, see pp. 46, 47.

The popular religion cannot do otherwise than take account of natural feeling.

So monotheistic theism, because it is the religion of the masses and at the same time under the spell of the Brahmanic world-view, finds itself faced by the task of gaining recognition for activity within world and life negation. It does not indeed demand any other activity than do the Brahmins. But it demands it in a different fashion. It cannot be satisfied, as are the Brahmins, to concede, alongside of renunciation of the world, a relative and limited justification to the activity naturally dictated by caste duty, but requires it to be service by which man so completely realises his self-devotion to God that it is of equal value with self-devotion to him in renunciation of the world.

In the esteem for activity to which monotheistic Hinduism was compelled as a popular religion, pre-historic Indian and ancient Aryan world and life affirmation rebelled against the Brahmanic world and life negation which originated in the thought of priests. Under the influence of the authority enjoyed by the Brahmanic world-view, Hinduism conceded the giving up of world and life affirmation in theory. But in practice it could not do so ; thus it was at variance with itself.

In this way was determined the course of the development it was destined to follow. Of necessity there must be a conflict between the world and life affirmation which, in its esteem for activity, it retained in practice and the world and life negation which it asserted in theory.

Originally, then, Hinduism had no intention of rebelling in any way against world and life negation.

It only wanted to gain recognition for activity within it. It thought it could combine a certain measure and a certain kind of world and life affirmation with world and life denial believed in as a principle.

But the reconciliation of the two which hovered before Hinduism was impracticable. As a matter of fact, every time the validity of world and life affirmation is established — even in cases limited to the justification of a certain action — it involves in a corresponding degree the putting out of action of world and life negation.

So this is what happens in Hindu thought—that world and life affirmation with ever increasing strength rises in rebellion against the world and life negation forced upon Indian thought by the Brahmins, and finally carries the day. But it does not accomplish this by its own intrinsic power. It only becomes capable of victory through the alliance it has made with ethics.

Neither ethics nor world and life affirmation, on its own account, can free itself from the fetters of Brahmanic world and life negation. With the Buddha a strongly developed ethic remains its prisoner. In ancient Hindu thought world and life affirmation, supported by the natural feeling of the people, similarly bows beneath world and life negation. But in the new Indian thought ethics and world and life affirmation join forces. It is only this ethical world and life affirmation that gets free from the delusion that world and life negation is an unassailable truth.

The chief sources of our knowledge of the mode of thought of the older Hinduism are the passages with religious-philosophic content which are introduced into the two great Indian epics, the Mahābhārata and the Rāmāyaṇa, and the Purāṇas. Purāna (really purāṇam ākhyānam) means old tale, so the Purāṇas contain myths and religious stories along with reflections upon them.

In the form in which they are preserved to us, the Mahābhārata and the Rāmāyaṇa belong to about the 2nd century A.D. In their earliest form they probably existed as early as the 4th century B.C. The material handled is of course still older.

The most ancient of the Purāṇas probably also go back to the 4th century B.C. if not still further.

The Hindu Bhakti religion may be older than Buddhism, but is certainly of later date than Brahmanic mysticism, to whose influence indeed it owes its rise. The beginning, then, of this higher development of popular religion may be referred to about 700 B.C.

That the Buddha makes no mention of the Bhakti religion does not indicate that it did not yet exist in his time. For the Buddha confines himself to a discussion of the various doctrines of world-renunciation and does not go into the question of popular religion.

* *
*

The first conflict between Hindu world and life affirmation and Brahmanic world and life negation is found in the famous Bhagavad-Gītā, a didactic poem interpolated in the Mahābhārata.

Mahābhārata (an abbreviation for Mahābhāratākhyānam) means the story of the great war of the Bharatas. The epic contains about 100,000 couplets and is the longest in all world-literature.

The action takes place in the neighbourhood of Delhi. The princes of the House of Bharata, who are already mentioned in the Vedic hymns, rule over the Kuru nation.

They are at enmity with their cousins, the five Pāndu Princes (Pāndavas) who share—and this proves the antiquity of the material of the epic—the beautiful Princess Draupadī as their wife.[1] Conspicuous among the Pāndavas are the justice-loving Yudhisthira, Bhīma the strong and Arjuna the skilled archer. The quarrel is to be decided by a game of dice. In the first game the Pāndavas lose to their opponents all they possess and, yet more, their joint wife, Draupadī. But as this ignominy is too great, the old blind King of the Kurus, Dhrtarāstra, cancels the game by allowing Draupadī to beg off herself and the five Pāndavas. In a second game the Pāṇḍavas lose again and must now pledge themselves to live twelve years with Draupadī in banishment in the jungle and pass a thirteenth unrecognised among men. When these years rich in adventure are past, they demand the return of their kingdom from the Kuru princes, but are met with a refusal. Finally they moderate their demand to five villages, but even these are not conceded. Now they declare war on their cousins. All the princes and heroes of the country round take sides for one party or the other. After a battle lasting eighteen days on the field of Kuru, which lies north of Delhi, the few survivors make peace and from that time onward govern their peoples as good neighbours. Later on they retire into solitude and die far from their countries.

*   *
*

This story fills only about half of the epic, the other half consisting of interpolated episodes: of tales related on one occasion or another, or songs of a didactic nature. Among the best-known and most beautiful of these tales are that of the noble King Nala, into

[1] Polyandry is said to be still found right up to the latest times among inhabitants of Tibetan origin of the southern (Indian) side of the Himalayas.

whom the demon of dice-playing enters, and his faithful wife Damayantī, and that of the Princess Sāvitrī, who takes for her spouse Prince Satyavant, who is living in solitude in the jungle, although she knows he must die after one year, and then successfully begs his life from the god of death. These two stories are among the most splendid creations of the literature of the world.

Among the interpolated didactic hymns of the Mahābhārata the first place belongs to the Bhagavad-Gītā (The Song of the Exalted One).[1] The exalted singer is Krishna, who appears as a manifestation of the god Vishnu. The Bhagavad-Gītā is one of the more ancient components of the Mahābhārata, and, apart from some later additions, may well date from the 3rd century B.C.

It may be assumed that it was originally an independent sacred text belonging to a Hindu brotherhood, and that it was only later worked into the Mahābhārata.

It is introduced at the beginning of the sixth book of the epic and precedes the description of the eighteen days' battle.

Before the battle the legitimate methods of warfare are agreed upon between the two parties. Only opponents of the same kind may engage against each other : charioteers only against charioteers, warriors mounted on elephants only against the like, cavalry only against cavalry, infantry only against infantry. The challenge of the opponent must precede the onset in due order. Those who surrender themselves prisoners, the disabled and those who are

[1] The complete title is " Bhagavadgītā-upaniṣadah ", that is to say, " The secret doctrines delivered by the Exalted One "

overtaken in flight may not be massacred. (This is also forbidden in the Laws of Manu.)

The drivers, beasts of burden, arms-bearers, musicians and in general all non-combatants must be free from attack.

Whilst the two armies face each other in readiness for battle, misgivings come to the hero Arjuna as to whether he ought to give the signal for battle between the two related clans and whether he can take upon himself the guilt of such murder. Undecided, his bow fallen from his hand, he sits in his war-chariot. Then Krishna, who serves as his charioteer, addresses him and instructs him that not only may he do this thing, but that he must do it.

So the Bhagavad-Gītā has to sift things to the very bottom. It is occupied not only with the general problem of the justification of action, but in addition with the special problem of the admissibility of non-ethical action. From the way in which it justifies action as such, there follows the possibility—and the necessity—of approving non-ethical action in certain circumstances.

*   *

*

CHAPTER XIII

THE BHAGAVAD-GĪTĀ

HOW then does the Bhagavad-Gītā justify activity within its world-view of world and life negation?

It professes without reservation the Brahmanic faith concerning the world. The world, says Krishna, has no meaning. It is only a play that God acts with himself. "By his magic power (Māyā) he makes all living creatures spin round like marionettes on their stage."

But Krishna will not admit the Brahmanic deduction that the man who has arrived at so much knowledge of the Universe ought to withdraw from the play and behave as an inactive, non-participant spectator of it. Incomprehensible as it is to him, he requires that he shall play his part in self-devotion to God in the play God has staged.

Krishna indeed does not utterly reject Brahmanic inactivity. "Giving up or carrying on one's work", he says, "both lead to salvation; but of the two, carrying on one's work is the more excellent."

It is not a matter of the external renunciation of action. "Neither does man attain to (the state of) being without work by undertaking no work, nor does he reach perfection by simply shunning the world." The true state of being without work is, he says, something inward and spiritual. Man must get to a point where he no longer accomplishes any act for the sake of expected advantage or enjoyment, or out of hatred or a spirit of revenge, like such as still live blindly in the world and seek satisfaction in it. If his heart has become free from the outward motives to action, he can perform any number of works; he will nevertheless remain in inactivity.

The Bhagavad-Gītā continued what the Buddha began. Drawing on his natural feeling, he rebelled against asceticism and self-torment and taught that the thing to strive after before all things is inner freedom from the world. The Bhagavad-Gītā does what he did not yet venture to do when it applies this manner of regarding things to the judgment of action as well. The supreme inactivity, it teaches, is when one performs actions as if one did not perform them.

In the light of the same perception that inner freedom from the world need not be outwardly demonstrated, Paul writes in the seventh chapter of the First Epistle to the Corinthians: " . . . they that have wives be as though they had none; And they that weep as though they wept not; and they that rejoice, as though they rejoiced not, and they that buy as though they possessed not ". For him, freedom from the world comes from faith in the approaching end of the world and beginning of the Kingdom of God. In outward demeanour still so to live in the world as existence in it involves, but inwardly to be liberated from it and feel oneself already at home in the Kingdom of God: it is this doctrine of the use of the world being still admissible that he opposes to the demand beginning to be voiced in his churches for outwardly expressed renunciation of the world.

According to Krishna, outward world and life

negation is not the will of God, and, further, is not practicable. For God himself practises activity in that he creates and maintains the Universe. How then can man desire to remain without works ? Let him admit that so long as he lives he cannot be one instant without activity. Krishna bids Arjuna reflect, " Thou canst not succeed even in preserving thy body, if thou art inactive " (Gītā, iii. 8).

The Bhagavad-Gītā therefore establishes the fact that world and life negation cannot get on without far-reaching concessions to world and life affirmation. Thence it draws the conclusion that man must once for all assume the right, which comprehends in itself all necessary concessions, of performing such actions as are requisite for the preservation of life and the fulfilment of natural duties.

The Bhagavad-Gītā takes up the Brahmanic thought of justification of action dictated by caste obligations, and develops from it the theory that activity and inactivity are equally justified.[1] If activity is required by the order of the Universe, it rightly concludes that there can be nothing that can be set above it. If God himself practises activity in creating and maintaining the Universe, then man also must devote himself to action.

With Brahmanic arguments the Bhagavad-Gītā wrests from Brahmanism the admission that activity and non-activity are equally justified. This means that the world and life affirmation which it claims recognises the sovereignty of world and life negation.

[1] On the view that action dictated by caste obligation is required by the divine order of the Universe and is in a certain sense excepted from world and life negation, see pp. 46, 47 ; 178, 179.

Krishna requires the outward performance of actions in combination with inward renunciation of the world. And when he speaks of action, he never means more than the exercise of the activity dictated by caste, not subjective action proceeding from the impulses of the heart and self-chosen responsibilities. If one would rightly understand the Bhagavad-Gītā, one must not forget the Brahmanic narrowness of its horizon.

* * *

Man must not be active for the sake of the fruits he expects from his work for himself and others. He must not be influenced by thinking of any aim that may be realised. He is to act solely from pure, absolute sense of duty with no empirical foundation.

Kant is not the first to lay down the doctrine of the Categorical Imperative. It had already been preached by Krishna in the words." Thy interest shall only be directed to the deed, never to the fruits thereof ". And whilst with Kant the content of absolute duty remains obscure, Krishna states it with exactitude. He defines it as the totality of the obligations which naturally belong to a man's station in life.

All work is to be done in loving self-surrender to God, because indeed it is God which worketh all in all.[1] Man must get rid of the illusion that his *ego* is the real worker. All that a man does is a happening sent by God. Krishna finds the reconciliation of the bondage and freedom of the will in the fact that man in spiritual self-surrender accomplishes what God does by means of him.

[1] See 1 Cor. xii. 6. [Translator's note.]

From the height of this mode of contemplation Krishna can also approve action which by human standards is judged evil. The ultimate question man has to ask himself is whether the work he resolves on comes to him as a task which must be fulfilled, and whether he accomplishes it in purest self-devotion to God. If he possesses this certainty, then he is free from any kind of guilt, even when he kills.

" One shall not absolve oneself from an obligation consequent on one's birth . . . even if it involves evil. For all undertakings are surrounded by evil as fire is surrounded by smoke " (Gītā, xviii. 48).

" Even if a thorough scoundrel loves me and nothing else (beside me), he must be deemed good; for he has well resolved " (Gītā, ix. 30).

" Even if thou wert the most sinful of all sinners, yet thou wouldst pass over all guilt with the boat of knowledge alone " (Gītā, iv. 36).

Krishna then dares to confess the simple truth that if the freedom of the will be denied, there can be no question of guilt.

On the ground of the instruction he thus, with many repetitions, delivers, he requires of Arjuna that he shall fight against his relations. He must recognise the fact that it is not he himself who kills, but that he only carries out a slaughter determined by God.

And furthermore he must take into consideration the fact that, according to true knowledge of Being, there is really no killing and no being killed. For only the transitory body, not the immortal *ego*, will be stricken by death.

" Even without thee, all the warriors who are standing in battle array will not remain (alive). . . . They are already beforehand slain by me : be thou merely the tool " (Gītā, xi. 32, 33).

" Just as man takes off worn-out clothes and puts on new ones, so does the spirit lay aside worn-out bodies and enter into others that are new " (Gītā, ii. 22).

" For whoever is born death is certain and similarly birth is certain for the dead. Therefore thou must not complain about a matter which is unavoidable " (Gītā, ii. 27).

" Is thy perplexity, which was due to want of knowledge, at an end ? " Krishna asks Arjuna when the instruction is finished. " My perplexity is at an end ", he replies and gives the signal for the battle.

* * *

When it became known in Europe at the end of the 18th and beginning of the 19th century, the Bhagavad-Gītā was welcomed with enthusiasm.[1] William von Humboldt devoted to it a long treatise in the Proceedings of the Academy of Berlin (1825–1826) and wrote in a letter to Fr. von Gentz (1827) : " It is probably the most profound and most sublime work the world can show "

The Bhagavad-Gītā made so great an impression on Europeans because by means of it they first became acquainted with a mysticism which promotes loving self-devotion to God in activity. It appeared to them to be a mysticism which corresponds to the European spirit of ethical Christian world and life affirmation, a mysticism, however, to which this spirit,

[1] In 1785 appeared the English translation by Charles Wilkins, and soon after a critical edition of the text by August Wilhelm von Schlegel, with a Latin translation. The first German translation is dated 1802.

hampered by the contemplative mysticism of Antiquity and the Middle Ages, had been unable to give birth.

But in reality the Bhagavad-Gītā has nothing of such a spirit. It is only an attempt undertaken by magnificent, unimpassioned thought to gain recognition for the idea of self-devotion to God by action within the world-view of world and life negation, and an attempt to prove that the man who stays at home and follows his calling is able to attain the same holiness and redemption as the monk who goes forth to homelessness and devotes himself to inactivity.

In the Bhagavad-Gītā world and life negation, after first disarming it, allows world and life affirmation to take a place beside itself on the throne. It grants recognition to activity, but only after activity has renounced natural motives and its natural meaning. By subtle tactics it renders its opponent harmless. It creates the conception of de-materialised action.

The charm of the Bhagavad-Gītā is due to this idea of spiritualised activity which springs only from the highest of motives.

But action which has ceased to be purposive in a natural way has lost its significance. The only activity which is truly of higher quality is that which sets natural aims before it and realises these in self-devotion to a supreme end.

All inner release from the world only draws its significance from the fact that by it we are rendered capable of the highest form of activity within the world.

In its fundamental thought the teaching of the

Bhagavad-Gītā is closely related to the speculative philosophy of J. G. Fichte (1762–1814). This too makes man take part in a play that God stages for Himself. According to Fichte, God, the Origin of Being, cannot rest in the state of pure Being because He is infinite Will-to-Action. Therefore he sets Himself a limitation of Himself in the material world in order to be constantly overcoming it and in order thereby to become conscious of Himself as Will-to-Action. Man then, as an individual divine *ego*, must see his destiny in endeavouring with this divine *ego* " to bring the whole world of the senses under the sovereignty of reason ".

Because he premises a world-view of ethical world and life affirmation, Fichte has to attribute the importance of ethical activity to the participation by man in the play staged by God. Therefore he ventures on the violent proceeding of defining ethics in quite general terms as the subjection of the world of the senses to reason. Starting from the conception of Divine activity which he has formed for himself, he gives human activity a meaning. In the Bhagavad-Gītā, on the other hand, man plays a part in the drama from a blind sense of duty, without seeking to find out its meaning, and, along with that, the meaning of his own action.

The relationship between the philosophy of Fichte and the Bhagavad-Gītā goes so far that Fichte too regards as the highest activity that by which man enters into the service of the order of the Universe. The duties which in his opinion stand in the front rank are not, as would be in harmony with the spirit of his age, the general duties based in the ethical nature of man, but those which result from his social position, his profession and his special endowments.

* *
*

The Bhagavad-Gītā stands in a curious relationship to ethics. The ethical and the non-ethical are found in it side by side.

Like the Buddha, if less forcibly, it demands an attitude of mind that is free from hatred and kindly as proof of inner freedom from the world. Hinduism has a far stronger interest in ethics than has the Brahmanic doctrine.

" He who hates no living creature, who is loving and compassionate, without selfishness and self-seeking, who holds pain and pleasure for equal, who is patient, contented, always loyal, full of self-control and steady determination, who fixes his mind and his reason on me and loves me, he is dear to me (Gītā, xii. 13, 14).

But Hinduism in the Bhagavad-Gītā does not yet take the actual step of demanding ethical deeds. Love to God is for it an end in itself. Hinduism does not make love to God find expression in love to mankind. Because it fails to reach the idea of active love, the ethic of the Bhagavad-Gītā is like a smoky fire from which no flame flares upward.

One must ever bear in mind, that in the Bhagavad-Gītā there is no question of loving self-devotion to the God of Love. God is for it a value completely exalted above good and evil. And because it desires active self-devotion to him, it reaches a point where it is forced to regard even non-ethical action as required by God.

Nothing of this kind comes into consideration

with Brahmanic mysticism. It allows man to be uplifted above good and evil in inactivity and absorbed into the One-and-All.[1] But it is a much more difficult matter for the mysticism of active self-devotion to the supra-ethical only God. This must be exalted above good and evil in action. Good and evil it must regard as something relative. And finally it can only judge the value of all action by the one criterion of whether it is accomplished in devotion to God or not.

If the mysticism of all periods contains some element of world negation, and ranks non-activity higher than activity, this goes back to the fact that the great problem is the mysticism of active union with infinite Being. In what way can man place himself at the service of a creative force which is an enigma to him? How can he combine the part of being the instrument of incomprehensible, supra-ethical necessity and at the same time of being an ethical personality? In the struggle for the true world-view as it is enacted in the thought of humanity, the ultimate question is always this—how can man, not only in thinking and in suffering, but also in acting, become one with infinite Being? And thought constantly endeavours to pass over the problem of the mysticism of action.

The great unknown thinker who unfolds his world-view in the Bhagavad-Gītā ventures to enter into discussion of the problem of the mysticism of action. He cannot avoid it, because in the world-view of world and life negation he cannot justify action as such, but only as performed in devotion to God. But in his mysticism of action he sees that he is compelled to renounce the complete maintenance of

[1] On this, see pp. 43, 44.

the difference between good and evil. This is the price he has to pay to obtain recognition for action within the world-view of world and life negation.

The Bhagavad-Gītā has a sphinx-like character.

It contains such marvellous phrases about inner detachment from the world, about the attitude of mind which knows no hatred and is kind, and about loving self-devotion to God, that we are wont to overlook its non-ethical contents. It is not merely the most read but also the most idealised book in world-literature.

* *
*

CHAPTER XIV

FROM THE BHAGAVAD-GĪTĀ TO MODERN TIMES

IN the Bhagavad-Gītā Hinduism wins its battle with Brahmanism for equality of spiritual rights by ingeniously harmonising its own world and life affirmation with Brahmanic world and life negation.

Then in the course of centuries it develops into a great religious power in India. It plays a far greater part than Brahmanism in thrusting back Buddhism. That which constitutes the strength of Buddhism, namely ethical inwardness, it possesses in equal degree, and it is superior to Buddhism in its popular religious mysticism. It allows people to remain in the religion to which they belong and lets them attain to perfection and redemption while living an active life.[1]

If India was able to maintain itself against Islam, by which it was threatened from the 11th century A.D. onward, the merit belongs in the first place to Hinduism.[2]

In the age of scholasticism the question was raised whether Hinduism could appeal to the testimony of the sacred texts in support of its claim to spiritual equality of rights with Brahmanism.

[1] For the reasons for the disappearance of Buddhism in India, see pp. 133-137.
[2] On the penetration of Islam into India, see p. 137.

Saṃkara (9th century A.D.), the great scholastic of Brahmanism, decided it by conceding that the Brahmanic doctrine and a doctrine covered by Hinduism are contained side by side in the Upanishads, the Brahmanic as the higher truth, the other as the lower.[1]

But the self-consciousness of Hinduism was by now so strongly developed that it could not be satisfied with the position thus accorded. The famous Hindu teacher Rāmānuja (1055–1137), in his great commentary on the Vedānta-Sūtras, maintained that neither these nor the Upanishads at all stand for the Brahmanic doctrine of union with the Brahman, but only for the Hindu doctrine of loving self-devotion to the one and only God. He conceived the Brahman as a personal God and identified it with Vishnu. In this of course he did violence to the texts. He had no understanding for the greatness of Brahmanic mysticism.

Hinduism does not lift itself above Brahmanism, but —after seating itself beside it in the Bhagavad-Gītā— usurps its place by reading its own doctrine both into the Brahmanic, and into the sacred texts. This process began with Rāmānuja and is still going on at the present day. Rabīndranāth Tagore is completing what Rāmānuja undertook to do.

The pure Brahmanic mysticism cannot maintain itself alongside of the Hindu because of its deficiencies as a world-view.. For it consists only in the certainty that man's immaterial *ego*, like all immaterial life which makes its appearance in the world of the senses, is one with the Universal Soul. And, in addition, the Brahmanic mysticism

[1] On this, see pp. 159-164

is difficult to uphold because it demands absolute detachment from the world and complete upliftedness above it. In Hindu mysticism, on the other hand, something happens between man and the highest Being. Man comes into living relationship with that Being and can even manifest his relationship in action without giving up his natural existence.

Brahmanic mysticism is marvellously simple and complete, but lifeless; Hindu mysticism is unfinished but alive. The living is always superior to the lifeless. So it comes about that in the course of time the pure Brahmanic mysticism gives place to a Hindu-Brahmanic mysticism in which the form is Brahmanic and the spirit Hindu.

* * *

As compared with the Bhagavad-Gītā, the ethical element gains in importance with Rāmānuja in so far as he no longer so obstinately emphasises the supra-ethical nature of God, but also tells of the kindness of God which brings friendly help to man. But he does not face the problem how God, the supra-ethical Primal Cause of the Universe, can at the same time be an ethical personality. The thought that love to God must be expressed in active love to mankind is just as far from him as from the Bhagavad-Gītā. Only, with him, divine love is already something warmer and more heartfelt than in the Bhagavad-Gītā.

The religious poets of the Mahratta country in south-west India sing of ardent divine love in hymns which are meant for use in the worship of Vishṇu. The most famous among them are Nāmdev (1270–1350 ?) and Tukārām (about 1608–1649).

When and how does the idea of active love to

mankind arise in Hindu thought beside that of loving self-devotion to God ?

It pushes its way into it gradually from popular ethics.

The fact that Brahmanism, Buddhism and ancient Hinduism teach no ethic of action does not mean that this was an unknown thing to the ancient Indians. Among the Indian people world and life affirmation and ethics are present. Wherever ethics reach a certain height in the presence of world and life affirmation, the idea of active love cannot fail to evolve. Among the Indians, just as among the Greeks, this ethic of subjective activity has difficulty in making its way alongside the ethic of duties demanded by society and objectively established by tradition and law. In some way or other, nevertheless, it does come into existence.

The case stands, then, thus—that the idea of active love is probably present somewhere in popular thought, but that Brahmanic, Buddhist and ancient Hindu thought cannot find room for it within their world-view! Because of the world and life negation which they represent, they cannot have anything to do with the world and life affirmation which is manifested in its greatest strength in the ethic of activity. Consequently the Bhagavad-Gītā restricts itself—which at first is so incomprehensible for us Europeans—to the justification of activity which is objectively necessary by reason of birth and caste. It believes, although in reality this does not hold good, that this concession to world and life affirmation is still compatible with the maintenance of world and life negation. But the world-view of world and life negation cannot acquiesce in subjective activity, especially not to the extent demanded by the ethic of love, without putting itself out of commission. This is the explanation of the exceedingly strange fact that through long centuries Indian thought remains so incomplete in the matter of ethics !

But finally it is nevertheless compelled by the popular ethic, which is developing without such hindrances, to concern itself with the ethic of active love and thereby to disregard the world-view of world and life negation. Of course it is Hinduism alone that is in the position to face this undertaking.

* *
*

That the idea of active love did arise in the popular ethics of India in fairly ancient times we know from many stories we meet in her literature and especially through the ethical maxims found in the Kural, a work which probably belongs to the 2nd century A.D.

The Kural is a collection of 1330 maxims in distich form, attributed to the weaver Tiruvalluvar. In the matter of authorship it is probable that not all the maxims are Tiruvalluvar's own, but that he also versified some which were ancient possessions of the people.

Kural means short strophe. Tiruvalluvar is really not a name, but a title borne by the religious teachers who work among the lower castes in the south of India.

The work is written in the Tamil language. This, like Canarese, which also belongs to the south of India, is an indigenous Indian language (Dravidian), not Indo-Aryan.

We know nothing certain about the life of Tiruvalluvar.

Legend reports that he was married, and that when a man inquired of him which is the right thing to do, to live as father of a family or as a hermit, he demonstrated the answer. He called his wife who happened to be at the spring. She left her water-jar hanging in the water and hurried to ask him what he wanted. When, according to Tamil custom, she set before him at breakfast cold rice left over from supper, he declared it was burning his tongue. She immediately blew on it to cool it. At midday he let something fall and called for a light to pick it up by. She straightway brought a lamp. Thereupon the inquirer said, " I have the answer! If so excellent a woman falls to one's share, the practice of domestic virtue is more excellent; otherwise it is better to become a hermit."

What a difference between the Kural and the Laws of Manu, which originated some four centuries before it! In the latter, under the dominance of the Brahmanic spirit, world and life affirmation is still just tolerated alongside world and life negation. In the Kural world and life negation is only like a distant cloud in the sky. In 250 maxims — they form the concluding part of the work—earthly love is lauded. Later times, because they cause offence, interpret them allegorically as concerning the love of the soul to God.

Christianity similarly interprets the Song of Solomon, a love-song probably originally sung at weddings and later absorbed into the Old Testament, as if it described the relations of the soul to its heavenly Redeemer.

In the ethics of the Kural, as in those of the Laws of Manu, the idea of reward has a place. The way of virtue is recommended because it leads to a better reincarnation or to liberation from re-birth. Alongside of this is found also the naïve view which is so conspicuous in Chinese ethics that moral behaviour results in earthly welfare and immoral in misfortune.

Nevertheless, ethics in the Kural are not so entirely dominated by the idea of reward as in Brahmanism, Buddhism and the Bhagavad-Gītā. We already find here the knowledge that good must be done for its own sake. It shines out from various maxims.[1]

" Even though one should say, There is no higher world, it is still good to give " (222).—" True liberality asks nothing in return. What does the world give in return to the cloud that gives it rain ? " (211).

Whilst the Bhagavad-Gītā in a forced and chilly manner gives as a motive for remaining in active life that it is in accordance with the order of the Universe, the Kural justifies it—what an advance !—by the idea of ethical activity. Work and profit place a man in a position to do good.

" All staying at home and waiting on the household have for their end hospitality and alms-giving " (81).—" All property gained by industrious toil is there for good men in order that they may practise well-doing " (212).

According to the Kural, duty is not confined, as in the Bhagavad-Gītā, to what the caste calling involves, but consists in general in " all that is good ".

Maxims about joy in activity, such as one would not expect from Indian lips, bear witness to the strength of the world and life affirmation present in the Kural.

" Even if fate did not permit of success : the striving in itself rewards the exertion of one's body " (619).—" If one accepts the burden as joy, there emerges a splendour for which even one's enemies are eager " (630).

[1] The quotations are from the German translation " Der Kurral " by Karl Graul, D.D., Leipzig 1856 (Derfling and Franke) and London 1856 (Williams and Norgate) (Bibliotheca Iamulica).

Like the Buddha and the Bhagavad-Gītā, the Kural desires inner freedom from the world and a mind free from hatred. Like them it stands for the commandment not to kill and not to damage.[1] It has appropriated all the valuable ethical results of the thought of world and life negation. But in addition to this ethic of inwardness there appears in the Kural the living ethic of love.

" The loveless man takes everything for himself ; the man full of love gives even his own bones to others " (72).—" The life of a soul without love is like the sprouting of a dried-up tree on stony ground " (78).—" What help can all the outer limbs give, if the inner limb of the body, love, is wanting ? " (79).—" If one weighs the value of the good deed done without consideration of the advantage : its kindness is greater than the ocean " (103).—" To assuage the deadly hunger of the poor is the treasury of the rich " (226).—" Wealth in benevolence is the wealth of wealths. Wealth in possessions the mob has also " (241).

With sure strokes the Kural draws the ideal of simple ethical humanity. On the most varied questions concerning the conduct of man to himself and to the world its utterances are characterised by nobility and good sense. There hardly exists in the literature of the world a collection of maxims in which we find so much lofty wisdom.

" If a kind man inherits property, it is as if a fruit-tree bears ripe fruit in the middle of a village " (216).—" The child ' Mercy ' born of love lives by the care of the well-to-do nurse ' Well-being ' " (757).—" The wealth of him who

---

[1] In opposition to the Buddha, the Kural decides that one may not eat meat even when one is quite innocent of the slaughter of the animal.

gives nothing to the poor is as if a very fine lady grows old in solitude " (1007).

" The gift is not the measure of the gift : its measure is in the magnanimity of the receiver " (105).

" Better than spending with a happy heart is to carry on sweet speech with a happy face " (92).—" For those who do not understand how to be friendly, the great wide world, even in bright daylight, lies in darkness " (999).

" Among all treasures that may be gained none can compare with attaining to freedom from envying any man " (162).

" To forget good is not good ; immediately to forget what is not good is good " (108).—" Holy as a penitent is he who forgets bitter speech from the lips of one who is excited " (159).

" Self-control leads to the immortals ; want of self-control rushes into thick darkness " (121).—" He who is not eager for pleasure, but knows that pain is natural, will remain free from distress " (628).

" Outward purity comes through water : purity of the heart is manifested in sincerity " (298).

" Those who are considerate and forbearing without letting their duty suffer : the world gladly gives itself to such " (578).—" The world rests on the excellence of the good prince who knows how to change enmity into friendship " (874).

" Even if they are highly placed, those who are not high-minded are not high ; even if their station be humble, those who are not low-minded are yet not low " (973).

" If thou dost harm to thy neighbour in the morning, harm comes of itself to thee in the afternoon " (319).

" Asking the way, happiness goes of itself to him who is undaunted in spirit " (594).—" Whoever says, ' I will work for my family ', before him there goes at once the goddess of good fortune, her robe well girded-up (*i.e.* as a fellow-worker) " (1024).

" Take no pleasure, even if thou shouldst win, in gambling. Even winning is as if a fish swallows the metal hook " (931).

"The friendship of well-conducted men waxes like the new moon: the friendship of fools wanes like the full moon" (782).

"Husbandmen are the axle-pin on the wagon of the world: they give support to all who, not caring for husbandry, are engaged in other work" (1032).

So a natural and ethical world and life affirmation of this kind was present among the people of India at the beginning of our era, although nothing of it can be found in Brahmanism, Buddhism and Bhagavad-Gītā Hinduism. It gradually penetrates into Hindu thought through the great religious teachers who had sprung from the lower castes and lived among and felt with the people.

* *
*

Another important influence on the development of the ethical in Hinduism was that within it, from the Middle Ages onward, Rāma, the through-and-through ethical god, began to enjoy the same veneration as Vishnu, Śiva and Krishṇa.

Rāma, like Krishna, is a national hero, who is later deified and finally regarded as a manifestation of Vishnu. He is the hero of the Rāmāyaṇa epic, attributed to the singer Vālmīki, which probably dates from the 4th century B.C.

The enlarged form in which we possess it—consisting of 24,000 couplets, and therefore compared with the Mahābhārata what Mount Pilatus is to Mount Everest—probably belongs to the 2nd century A.D.

The Rāma Saga itself is of course much older. Its home is north-east India, in the Kosala country, that is to say in the region in which Buddhism originated.

Rāma is the favourite son of King Daśaratha, and as the

King feels death approaching is about to be installed by him as his successor. But one of his wives, Kaikeyī by name, requires of him that he shall choose her son by him, Bharata. As he had once promised her the fulfilment of two wishes, he must conform to her will in this and in addition banish Rāma for fourteen years. Rāma willingly acquiesces in both matters in order that his father may keep his word so blindly given in earlier days. His faithful wife Sītā—the name means *furrow*—follows him into the jungle. After the death of the King, Bharata, Kaikeyī's son, comes to him contrite and begs him to take over the sovereignty. But Rāma refuses. He must fulfil his father's command. And now Sītā is carried off from the jungle by the demon Rāvaṇa, who conveys her through the air to the island of Lankā in the ocean (probably Ceylon is meant) where he rules as king in human form. But she refuses to become his wife. Thereupon he imprisons her in a grove and threatens to slay her if she does not change her mind within a year.

Rāma learns the whereabouts of his wife through the clever Monkey-King, Hanumat, a son of the Wind-god. Hanumat goes forth to search for news, flies southward, reaches the sea, in four days crosses to the island through the air, transforms himself into a cat and finds his way to the prisoner. From her he learns what threatens her and that the respite allowed will be up in two months. He returns to Rāma and in haste starts with him and a great army of monkeys to attack the island. Within a few days the monkeys build a bridge of rocks and trees across the ocean. Rāvana's city is besieged, and after severe struggles its conquest is accomplished. Rāma kills Rāvaṇa in single combat and returns with Sītā to his kingdom, the fourteen years having meanwhile come to an end.

According to the later form in which we possess the romantic epic—it probably belongs to the 2nd century A.D. —Rāma is identical with Vishnu. As the demon Rāvana is dangerous to the gods but can only be fought by men,

Vishnu consents to be born as a son of King Daśaratha in order to destroy him.

Devotion in love to Rāma is taught by Rāmānanda (about A.D. 1400), who belongs to the school of Rāmānuja.[1] But in his mysticism ethics already play a much greater part than in that of his predecessor. In Rāmānanda at last the thought is developed that devotion to God must be manifested in love to man. He conceives God as an ethical personality.

Through his demand for all-embracing love among mankind Rāmānanda arrives at no longer observing caste distinctions. In his endeavour for the recognition of the human dignity and human rights of the poorest and most despised of the people, we see what significance ethics were beginning to acquire in Hinduism.

Rāmānanda came from the south and worked in the north, and through him the spirit of the south won great influence over that of the north. Although he had grown up in the knowledge of Sanskrit he expressed his thoughts in Hindi, that they might become the property of the people; and he bade his pupils do likewise.

He had twelve pupils. Among them were two women, a man who was a Pariah and two Moslems. In his broadmindedness he gave even to them sayings from the Veda as sacred mottoes to guide their lives.

In his free poetical rendering of the Rāma Epic called Rām-carit-mānas or " The Sea of the Deeds of Rāma ", written in the Hindi vernacular of eastern

[1] For Rāmānuja, see pp. 197, 198.

India, the famous poet Tulsī-Dās (1532–1624) glorifies love to Rāma and at the same time holds him up before men as a moral example. Tulsī-Dās teaches the brotherhood of all men and attributes fatherly kindness to the god, Rāma.

The most distinguished disciple of Rāmānanda was the weaver Kabīr (1440–1518) who worked in north-east India in the Gorakhpore district. Influenced by Islam, in which he grew up, he criticised the Hindu toleration of polytheism.

During the wars which the inhabitants of northern India waged against the Mohammedan rulers, the religious fellowship which originated with Kabīr and his great pupil Nānak from Lahore (1469–1539) was organised into the political theocracy of the Sikhs. Sikh means *disciple* or *learner*.

Through mysticism Kabīr and Nānak were uplifted above the differences between Islam and Hinduism. A spirit of deep humility towards God dominates their mysticism.

The attempt of Akbar the Great (1542–1605), the ruler of the dynasty of Tamerlane who occupied the throne of Delhi from 1556 to 1605, to form a universal religion out of Hinduism, Buddhism, Islam (which he abjured in 1582) and the religion of Zarathustra, with the aid of Christianity, with which he had become acquainted through Portuguese missionaries, is well known. What he founded failed to last.

*   *

*

CHAPTER XV

MODERN INDIAN THOUGHT

IN modern times, then, ethical world and life affirmation in Hinduism becomes more and more significant. This development is associated with the names of Rām Mohan Ray (1772–1833), Debendranāth Tagore (1817–1905), Keshab Chandra Sen (1838 – 1884), Dayānand Sarasvatī (1824 – 1883), Rāmakrīshṇa (1834–1886), Svāmin Vivekānanda (1862 – 1902), Rabīndranāth Tagore (*b.* 1861), Mahatma Gandhi (*b.* 1869) and Aurobindo Ghose (*b.* 1872).

That these men undertook more energetically than any of their predecessors to combine with the ethic of becoming more perfect of heart the ethic which seeks activity within the world is, of course, due to the fact that they had become acquainted with, and influenced by, modern European world and life affirmation and the Christian ethic of love. But this stimulus from without only set in motion a process of development which had already begun independently.

Rām Mohan Ray (1772–1833), born of a Bengali Brahmin family, devoted himself to research into all religions and was deeply impressed by the personality and message of Jesus. In 1820 he published a book about His teaching (*The Precepts of Jesus*), which in his opinion contains ideas to which Indian thought does not ascribe sufficient importance. But at the same time he was convinced that these ideas can also be found in the Upanishads, if only they be rightly expounded. In the Upanishads, therefore, which he regarded as the highest revelation, he discovered the doctrine of the ethical divine personality and the self-devotion to it which is expressed in active love to mankind. He, the Brahmin, interpreted Brahmanic mysticism and the sacred writings in an ethical sense and believed that in this way he was restoring its original purity to the Indian doctrine. So his exposition of the Upanishads does them even more violence than does that of Rāmānuja.

Rām Mohan Ray came forward as the reformer of the Hinduism which claimed to be the true Brahmanism. In the year 1828 he founded the Brāhma Samāj (Society of Believers in the Brahman) an association designed to foster the loftiest religion. It became very important and endures down to the present day.[1] Its members belong principally to the higher circles of the population of Bengal.

Rām Mohan Ray was the great pioneer of modern Indian thought. His knowledge of the religions of the world was remarkable, as was also his linguistic ability, for he knew Bengali, Sanskrit, Persian, Arabic, English, Greek and Hebrew.

At that time it was an unheard-of thing for an Indian to be in touch with and make a serious study of European learning and philosophy. So orthodox Brahmins attacked Rām Mohan Ray with the greatest vehemence. Only so powerful a personality as he

[1] At first the association bore the name Brāhma Sabhā.

was could have undertaken to defy their threats of terrorism.

He devoted himself earnestly to social reform and dared to advocate the abolition of Sati (the burning of widows) and other customs irreconcilable with the demands of ethics.[1] As a result of his propaganda, in the year 1829 the British Government could venture to forbid widow-burning. He also spoke openly against caste, but at the same time he took precautions that at the meetings for divine service held every Saturday by the Brāhma Samāj the Vedic texts should not be recited in the presence of members of the lower castes !

In the year 1830 he went to England. His chief motive for the journey was that the law against widow-burning was in danger of being abrogated on account of the opposition organised against it by the Brahmins.

During his stay he met Jeremy Bentham (1748–1832), the venerable but still fiery prophet of the rational love of mankind, and was saluted by him as " an admired and beloved fellow-worker in the service of humanity ". He died on the 27th September 1833 at Bristol and lies buried there.

*   *
   *

Debendranāth Tagore (1817–1905), equally a scion of a Bengal Brahmin family, continued the work of Rām Mohan Ray.[2] He organised the Brāhma

[1] For the origin of the custom of burning widows, see p. 171.
[2] Tagore is an anglicised form of the Bengali name, Thākur.

Samāj, and drew up for it a kind of confession of faith (1843).

God is a personal being with sublime moral attributes.—God has never become incarnated.—God hears and answers prayer.—God is to be worshipped only in spiritual ways. Hindu asceticism, temples and fixed forms of worship are unnecessary. Men of all castes and races may worship God acceptably.—He requires no worship but desires reverence of spirit.—Repentance and cessation from sin is the only way to forgiveness and salvation.—Nature and Intuition are the sources of knowledge of God.—No book is authoritative.[1]

Unlike the strict Brahmins, Debendranāth Tagore did not regard the Upanishads as inspired. Nevertheless they were for him the source of highest truth.

In the year 1848, influenced by the English Book of Common Prayer, he compiled a collection of texts from the Upanishads, the Laws of Manu, the Mahābhārata and other writings held to be sacred. These elucidate and complete his confession of faith.

It was for him a matter of course that love for God must be proved by love to mankind. But he did not introduce this maxim into his confession of faith.

Keshab Chandra Sen (1838-1884), a member of a Bengal doctor's family, was at first one of Debendranāth Tagore's adherents. But later on he became the representative of a doctrine whose position in relation to Brahmanic tradition was even freer than his was. His aim was the construction of a universal religion which should comprise in itself all historical

---

[1] See *Hastings' Encyclopædia of Religion and Ethics*, ii. p. 816, J. N. Farquhar, 1850.

religions. Whilst Debendranāth Tagore only made use of the sacred writings of India, Keshab Chandra Sen compiled for his followers a volume of devotion (1866) drawn from Hindu, Buddhist, Christian, Mohammedan and Chinese texts. He even changed the day for worship to Sunday. European-Christian influence manifested itself in him so strongly that in his confession of faith he calls God the Father of all men instead of the Father of all that lives, as, being an Indian, he should.

He laid great importance on active ethics. A journey to England (1869–1870) further increased his zeal for social work.

In the last years of his life the rational and the ethical gave place more and more to the Indian mystical. He once more ascribed importance to the popular faiths and again attributed great value to the experience of union with God in ecstasy.

Dayānand Sarasvatī (1824–1883), whose real name was Mūl Śaṅkar, was born of a Brahmin family engaged in business.

It is possible that he took the name Sarasvatī from the blind Guru (teacher) Virajanand Sarasvatī whom he regarded as his real father after he became estranged from his own father because he would not join in polytheistic worship and had, in 1845, finally left his parents' home.

The course of his development was determined by Debendranāth Tagore and Keshab Chandra Sen. Later on (1881) he broke away from them.

His activity centred in north-west India. Here he gained adherents for the association he founded in 1875 known as the Ārya Samāj (community of the Āryas), a parallel society to the Brāhma Samāj. What characterises the Ārya Samāj is the energetic fashion in which the practice of active love in the interest of the welfare of society is enjoined on its members as a duty.

From the ten articles of the Creed of the Ārya Samāj :
" The primary object of the Samāj is to do good to the world, by improving the physical, spiritual and social condition of mankind."
" All ought to be treated with love and justice and due regard to their merits."
" Ignorance ought to be dispelled and knowledge diffused."
" No one ought to be contented with his own good alone, but everyone ought to regard his prosperity as included in that of others." [1]

By " Āryas " Dayānand Sarasvatī did not so much understand the members of a race as noble-minded people in general. He determined accordingly that members of all castes could become members of the Ārya Samāj. And according to him all those who have the mentality of Āryas are entitled to study the holy scriptures and are qualified to expound them during divine service. Debendranāth Tagore had held fast to the rule that this must remain a privilege of those who were Brahmins by birth.

Dayānand Sarasvatī also advocated permitting marriage between members of different castes, while he opposed child-marriage.

In the number of its adherents—which reaches several hundred thousand—and in the weight of its

[1] See J. N. Farquhar, *Modern Religious Movements in India*, 1918, p. 120.

influence the Ārya Samāj is greater far than the Brāhma Samāj.

Dayānand believed he must and could derive his doctrine—a doctrine which is interwoven with the spirit of freedom and progress—entirely from the Veda. Among the Articles of the faith of the Ārya Samāj we find, " The Veda is the book of all true knowledge ".

But this applies only to the four original and most venerable parts (Samhitās) of the Veda, the Rig-Veda, the Sāma-Veda, the Yajur-Veda and the Atharva-Veda. All later scriptures, beginning with the Brāhmaṅas, even if they are reckoned as belonging to the Veda, fail, according to Dayānand, to contain the original revelation itself, and contain only human expositions and explanations which are valuable indeed but in part overgrown with error.[1]

Not merely all true religion, but every kind of knowledge in general, is contained, according to Dayānand, in the original Veda. All scientific discoveries that have been made and remain to be made are indicated in it. There is complete agreement between the revelation of God in Nature and the revelation in the Veda. Even the system of the Universe as described by Copernicus may already be found in the Veda.

In the arts of exegesis therefore Dayānand was far in advance of Rāmānuja and all his successors. He deserves great appreciation for his work on behalf of school education and the spread of learning.

His followers declared that he was poisoned by his

[1] For the four original parts (Saṃhitās) of the Veda, see p. 21 ; for the later parts p. 33.

cook at the instigation of the concubine of a prince whom he had blamed for his manner of living.

*   *
  *

Rāmakrishna (1834–1886), whose real name was Gadādhar Chatterji, was the son of a poor Brahmin family of Bengal. Even as a child he experienced states of ecstasy. At the age of twenty he became a priest at a shrine of the great goddess Kālī near Calcutta, and there he served for ten years. Later he led the life of a wandering friar.

A nun of Brahmin origin and an aged ascetic had great influence over him. The ascetic initiated him into the Vedānta doctrine. In a vision he experienced the union with Krishna for which he had yearned so long. Later he studied the Bhakti doctrine, and also made acquaintance with Islam and Christianity. From that time he saw in Jesus, as in Krishṇa and in the Buddha, an incarnation of the Divine. In ecstasy he was united to Him.

Although he was acquainted with Debendranāth Tagore and Dayānand Sarasvatī he entered into no close relations with them. For Keshab Chandra Sen, on the other hand, he cherished a deep veneration which was fully reciprocated. Keshab Chandra Sen recognised the greatness of the monk in spite of his being ignorant of Sanskrit and scarcely able to write, and directed the attention of the large circle of his own followers to him. Before this he had only been known to a few. Each of the two personalities, so different from each other, mutually gave much and received much. Rāmakrishna sympathised with the endeavours of the Brāhma Samāj.

One of the last visits received by Keshab when he was dying was from Rāmakrishna.

In his childlike humility Rāmakrishna is akin to Francis of Assisi. To kill the last stirrings of caste pride in himself he would undertake the most menial tasks.

This mystic, who found such delight in the experience of ecstasy, was inspired also by a spirit of warmest love for his fellows.

" Oh Mother," he entreats the goddess Kālī, whom he deeply reverenced to the end of his life, " let me remain in contact with mankind ; let me not become a hard ascetic."

For him there were no questions of dogma. He decided the question whether personality is to be ascribed to God or not by saying that men imagine Him according to their natural gifts as a personality or as non-personal.

In thorough Hindu fashion Rāmakrishna judged that God Himself is somehow or other present in an image and draws to Himself the worship given to it.

He did not trouble about the universal religion comprising all religions within itself with which Debendranāth Tagore, Keshab Chandra Sen and Dayānand Sarasvatī were concerned. What men believe he held to be of secondary importance. Piety is all that matters. Every religion, whatever its doctrine, becomes the true religion when man dedicates himself in love to God and serves his neighbour in love. So there is no sense in exchanging one religion for another. Union with God should be sought by the Christians in Christianity, by the Mohammedans in Mohammedanism and by the Hindus in Hinduism.

* * *

The most distinguished disciple of Rāmakrishna was Svāmin Vivekānanda (1862–1902), whose real name was Narendra Nāth Datta. He was born of a good Calcutta family of the Kśatriya (warrior) caste. In his youth he became familiar with Indian scholarship and made some acquaintance with the philosophy and science of Europe. He first met Rāmakrishna as a boy of 17 in 1880, but did not immediately come under his influence. His rationalistic mind, influenced by reading John Stuart Mill, Herbert Spencer and Keshab Chandra Sen, adopted a critical attitude towards Rāmakrishna's mystical piety. But little by little Rāmakrishna's great personality won power over him, especially from the time when he had to struggle with the cares and stress of life. For after the sudden death of his father (1884), who had not managed to live within his means, it was discovered that the family was completely ruined. Narendra had to come to an understanding with the creditors and endeavour to earn a living to support his mother and brothers. From despair and rebellion against God, who permits misery to take its course in the world, he wrestled his way through to the peace which rests on faith, and from this starting-point learned to understand the piety of Rāmakrishna. Along with the change in heart the state of ecstasy gained for him a significance which he shared with the Master.

But Rāmakrishna, familiar as he was with the state of ecstasy, did not regard such a naturally experienced union with the Absolute as the most to be desired and highest of all experiences. He recognised that a piety which is concerned only with the *ego* and its absorption into the Infinite is in danger of becoming egoistic and therefore valueless. So he forced himself to keep his thoughts directed to service within the world and made that also the duty of his favourite disciple. He opposed Vivekānanda's project when he wanted to follow the example of his paternal grandfather, who at the age of twenty-five had left his wife and children and a high position in order to become a hermit. He impressed on him again and again that he was in the world to bring the true faith to man and to serve the poor and the wretched in the spirit of love. And Vivekānanda obeyed him.

What is great in Rāmakrishna and Vivekānanda is that both experience and enjoy the state of ecstasy and yet are superior to it and draw their final criterion for the judgment of spiritual matters from ethical thought.

After the Master's death, Vivekānanda lived a wandering life for several years, in the course of which he became familiar with nearly the whole of India. When he learned that on the occasion of the World Fair in Chicago there was to be a congress of all religions he resolved, in 1892, to attend it. On this journey he was pursuing a twofold object : he wanted to preach to the world the sublime knowledge of which India is the guardian and he wanted to collect in the wealthy countries of Europe and America the material means to alleviate the misery and poverty of India which on his travels he had learned to realise.

It was at the moment of his departure for America that he assumed the name Vivekānanda.

At the congress (September 1893) in a glowing speech he developed the thought of Rāmakrishṇa that true piety is to be found in all religions and is higher than them all.

After the congress he stayed on for over three years in America and Europe in order to make the Vedānta doctrine known. The social work accomplished in both continents compelled his admiration. But he did not penetrate far enough into Western thought to be able to establish relations with it and realise its right value.

In the year 1897 he returned to India and summoned the inhabitants of that great empire to social activity. In May of the same year, with the aid of Rāmakrishna's other disciples, he founded the Rāmakrishna Mission. This was to make the Master's ideas known in India and throughout the world, to labour for the re-birth of India and to organise a service of love for the poor and wretched of the land.

In the spirit of the Master, Vivekānanda laid down the principle that religion must be a religion of action. He ventured on such axioms as that the best religion consists in seeing Siva in all human beings and especially in the poor, and that he alone worships God who helps and serves all living things. That the original pure religion of the Veda was this religion of love was for him a firmly established fact.

Basing his arguments loosely on the Bhagavad-Gītā, which he interpreted in accordance with the higher ethic he had reached, he taught that the soul can realise its unity with God by knowledge and self-submergence (Rajayoga) no less than by activity in duty and love (Karmayoga).

Vivekānanda was an impetuous innovator in the struggle against what was old, in so far as it was socially injurious. On the other hand, he stood, like Rāmakrishṇa, for the maintenance of the popular Hindu faith and worship, because in these the people symbolically possessed and made active the doctrine of union with the Universal.

From June 1899 to December 1900, weary and with health already undermined (he suffered from diabetes), he undertook a second tour in Europe and America. It was a grievous disappointment to him. He found in Western civilisation much less that was good and admirable than on his previous visit, and could not understand how it was that in many respects he had set so high a value upon it. He was more than ever convinced that to satisfy their spiritual and mental needs Europe and America must turn to what India has to offer them.

On 4th July 1902, at the age of thirty-nine, he passed peacefully away.

For us people of the West the great spiritual and ethical personality of Vivekānanda is rendered difficult to understand by what appears to us his boundless self-consciousness and by the hard, unjust and contradictory judgments in which he allowed himself to indulge.

The work he founded, the Rāmakrishṇa Mission, still exists and is very effectual for good.

* *

*

It is remarkable that the problem of deliverance from re-birth passes altogether into the background in modern Indian thought. The idea of mystical union with God ceases to be so intimately connected with the idea of reincarnation as was still the case, for example, in the Bhagavad-Gītā. The fear of re-incarnation no longer plays the part it did in the Buddha's time. Union with God is again striven after for its own sake. And thus Indian mysticism again attains to its old spontaneity and freedom. It is true that it does not expressly assert its immunity from the idea of transmigration under whose dominion it had lived for centuries, but it ceases to be ruled by it.

From the moment when the mysticism of self-devotion to God in ethical activity appears side by side with the mysticism of union with Him through knowledge and self-submergence—from that moment the position of the doctrine of reincarnation is shaken. Up to then ethics were only considered in relation to reincarnation. By right action one could only attain to a better reincarnation, not to union with God. But now, in measure as the ethical finds acceptance in the mysticism of union with God, the idea of reincarnation loses its significance. In modern Indian thought therefore the process that had been accomplished under the pressure of natural necessity is completed.

Nevertheless, Indian thought could not abandon the idea of reincarnation, for it had been handed down by tradition and by means of it a natural connection had been established between world and life negation and world and life affirmation. By reason of the idea of reincarnation Indian thought can be reconciled to the fact that so many people in their minds and actions are still so engrossed in the world. If we assume that we have but one existence, there arises the insoluble problem of what becomes of the spiritual *ego* which has lost all contact with the Eternal. Those who hold the doctrine of reincarnation are faced by no such problem. For them that non-spiritual attitude only means that those men and women have not yet attained to the purified form of existence in which they are capable of knowing the truth and translating it into action.

So the idea of reincarnation contains a most comforting explanation of reality by means of which Indian thought surmounts difficulties which baffle the thinkers of Europe.

* *
*

Rām Mohan Ray, Debendranāth Tagore, Keshab Chandra Sen, Dayānand Sarasvatī, Rāmakrishna and Vivekānanda stood for the furtherance of love in action without troubling about the question whether and how this ethical world and life affirmation could be united with their mysticism of world and life negation. They professed certain opinions without systematically thinking out and defining the world-view which corresponds with those opinions.

Hinduism possesses an astonishing capacity for overlooking or setting aside theoretical problems because from time immemorial it has lived in a state of compromise between monotheism and polytheism, between pantheism and theism, between world and life negation and world and life affirmation, and between supra-ethical and ethical ways of regarding things. It does not go to the root of the questions with which it is concerned, but is only intent on finding practical, satisfying solutions. Mixing up old and new, it constructs a world-view out of what it regards as true and valuable, but it does not attempt to give it a real foundation. It holds that to be unnecessary. If this particular world-view is valuable because of the convictions it comprises, that is sufficient proof for Hinduism that it is right.

So Rām Mohan Ray, Debendranāth Tagore, Keshab Chandra Sen, Dayānand Sarasvatī, Rāmakrishna and Vivekānanda endeavour rather to further the development of the Hindu world-view, than attempt to base it in reality. That is why they fail to realise that by their profession of the ethic of love in action they cut themselves loose from world and life negation. They think they can give Brahmanic mysticism a fresh interpretation in an ethical and life-affirming sense, just as if a piece of music written in the minor could be changed into the major key. As a matter of fact they have encountered the tremendous problem of ethical and world and life affirming mysticism.

It is partly because they live under the influence of the authority of tradition that they are satisfied with compromise instead of really getting to the bottom of the problems of world-view. They do not like to confess to themselves that they are the representatives of intuitions and convictions which had not yet found expression when the Upanishads and other sacred books were composed. So that is why they endeavour to find their ideas in the ancient texts. But the only way they can succeed in this is by using all their skill in reading meanings into them which are not really there.

The sufferings of the New Testament at the hands of its interpreters are certainly not trifling. But the sufferings of the Vedic hymns and the Upanishads are far, far worse.

Modern Indian thought is still without right feeling for concrete truth and truth based on reality because it has not yet attained to freedom.

* *
*

The philosophy of Mahatma Gandhi is a world in itself.

Born at Porbandar in 1869, Gandhi is a member of the Vaiśyā Caste, the caste of merchants and agriculturists. After attending Indian schools up to his eighteenth year, he came to London to study Law. In 1893 an Indian firm sent him to South Africa to settle a lawsuit, and there he became acquainted with the conditions under which the Indian immigrants were living. He settled in the country as a lawyer and up to 1914 was the leader of his countrymen in their struggles for their rights. As his method of warfare he chose passive resistance, and it proved successful. In the Boer War (1899) he joined up with other Indians as a volunteer in the Ambulance Service. When the Great War broke out he was in London and took part in the formation of an ambulance column of Indian volunteers. But at the end of the year 1914 he was obliged to return to India on account of his health, and there he began to study the economic and political problems of his home country. The cause he made his own was the liberation of the Indian labourers who had emigrated to the colonies from the regulation, which had the force of law, that they must be bound by a five years' contract. He fought also for the abolition of abuses on the indigo plantations in Northern India. He became the representative of the rights of the operatives in spinning factories in Ahmedabad who were at variance with their masters, and of the peasants of the Khaira district, who had got into debt through the failure of their harvest, when they were in conflict with the taxation authorities. By threatening or organising passive resistance he always succeeded in gaining recognition for the demands he represented.

When the War was over (1919) he had recourse to similar methods to prevent the passing of exceptional laws against political agitators (the so-called Rowlatt Bills), but discovered that passive resistance in the Panjāb led to violent revolutionary movements which were suppressed by the authorities with great severity. He was also disappointed that the British Government did nothing after the war to preserve the throne of the Sultan at Constantinople whom the Indian Mohammedans regarded as their religious overlord. In his endeavour to bring about an agreement between the Hindus and Mohammedans he had made the claims of the latter his own.

In 1920 in common with the Hindu and Mohammedan popular leaders he formed the momentous resolve to give up co-operation with the British Government. In the course of the passive resistance movement to champion the idea of the independence of the Indian people and promote the boycott of imported factory-made materials in favour of the resuscitation of Indian hand-spinning and hand-weaving, serious disturbances occurred in Bombay and Chauri Chaura. As the originator of civil resistance to the authority of the State, Gandhi was condemned to six years' imprisonment, but after some time (1924) he was pardoned. In the years that followed the enmity which had broken out afresh between Hindus and Mohammedans caused him great grief.

In recent years, withdrawn from politics, he has devoted himself mainly to the question of the social and ethical education of the people. In the forefront of the reforms that must be achieved he places the removal of the existing prejudices against members of the lowest castes, the so-called Untouchables, who number some fifty millions; the abolition of child marriage; the recognition of the principle that women should have equal rights with men; and the complete control of alcohol and poisonous drugs.

Never before has any Indian taken so much interest in concrete realities as has Gandhi. Others were for the most part contented to demand a charitable attitude to the poor. But he—and in this his thought is just like that of a modern European—wants to change the economic conditions that are at the root of poverty.

Ninety per cent of the population of India live in villages. During the dry season, which lasts for about six months of the year, work on the land is at a standstill. Formerly the people made use of this time for spinning and weaving. But since materials manufactured outside India as well as in Indian factories have governed the market, these home industries have been ruined. It is because the villagers have lost their former income from these secondary occupations that there is so much poverty in country districts. And the idleness involved has disastrous results.

Gandhi preaches a healthy feeling for reality when he tries to make it possible for the villagers to take up their hand-spinning and hand-weaving once more and tells them that it is their duty to do so. He rightly sees that here we have the preliminaries of a competition between hand-work and machine-work and that the development of the situation must be guided as far as possible in the interest of the people.

Gandhi is no blind enemy of machines. In so far as they are necessary he gives them their due. But he will not agree to their ruining a manual industry which in itself is capable of survival. He has great appreciation for the sewing-machine, but he still rejects the motor-car although, as promoting intercourse between one village and another, it is in many respects the natural ally of home industries.

His programme of village reform also includes the provision of better dwellings and better hygienic conditions, and the introduction of rational methods of farming.

The first impulse to the high esteem in which he holds bodily labour and the way of life of the agriculturist and artisan came to him from Ruskin's *Unto This Last*, which he read while he was living in South Africa. He confesses that this book caused an immediate change in his view of life.

Gandhi's feeling for reality is seen also in his relations to the Ahimsā commandment. He is not satisfied with praising it, but examines it critically. He is concerned at the fact that in spite of the authority of this commandment there is in India such a lack of pity both for animals and mankind. He ventures to say, " I hardly think that the fate of animals is so sad in any other country in the world as it is in our own poor India. We cannot make the English responsible for this ; nor can we excuse ourselves by pleading our poverty. Criminal neglect is the only cause of the deplorable condition of our cattle ".

The fact that the Ahimsā commandment has not educated the people to a really compassionate attitude he attributes to its having been followed more in the letter than in the spirit. People have thought they were obeying it sufficiently by avoiding killing and the causing of pain, while in reality the commandment is only fulfilled by the complete practice of compassion.

It is not clear to Gandhi that it belongs to the original nature of the Ahiṃsā commandment only to demand abstinence from killing and hurting, and not the complete exercise of compassion. He took upon himself to go beyond the letter of the law against killing, and this moreover in a case where he came into conflict with the Hindu reverence for horned cattle. He ended the sufferings of a calf in its prolonged death-agony by giving it poison. By this act he caused his Hindu adherents no less offence than when for the first time he received untouchables at his settlement (Ashram).

Thus in Gandhi's ethical life affirmation Ahimsā is

freed from the principle of non-activity in which it originated, and becomes a commandment to exercise full compassion. It becomes a different thing from what it was in the thought of ancient India.

And through his feelings for reality Gandhi also arrives at the admission that the commandment not to kill and not to injure cannot be carried out in entirety, because man cannot maintain life without committing acts of violence. So with a heavy heart he gives permission to kill dangerous snakes and allows the farmer to defend himself against the monkeys which threaten his harvest.

It is one of the most important of Gandhi's acts that he compels Indian ethics openly to come to grips with reality.

So great is his interest in what is worldly that he also has sympathy with sports and games. He demands that in the schools as much time should be given to bodily exercises as to the training of the mind, and laments that in his boyhood there were no games, so that he had to be contented with long walks up hill and down dale. So in one corner his world and life affirmation is marked " Made in England ".

But with this feeling for and interest in what is real, there is united in him a purely immaterial idea of what activity is. For him it is an established principle that material problems can only be solved by the Spirit. He is convinced that since all that happens in human affairs is conditioned by mind, things can only be improved by bringing about a different state of mind. So, in all that we undertake, we must be careful to make our own mind influence other minds. According to him the only real forces at our disposal are the spirit of freedom from hatred and the spirit of love. He regards the belief that worldly ends must be pursued by worldly methods as the fatal error which is responsible for the misery which prevails on this earth.

Gandhi continues what the Buddha began. In the Buddha the spirit of love set itself the task of creating different spiritual conditions in the world; in Gandhi it undertakes to transform *all* worldly conditions.

And according to Gandhi, political activity as well must be governed by the spirit of Ahimsā. " For me ", he wrote in a letter, " there are no politics that are not at the same time a religion."

But is the passive resistance of which Gandhi makes such abundant use to realise his objects really a non-worldly method, derived from the spirit of Ahimsā, of championing the cause of good in the world against its opponents ? Only partly so.

In themselves, Ahimsā and passive resistance are two quite different things. Only Ahimsā is non-worldly; passive resistance is worldly.

The ancient Indian Ahimsā is an expression of world and life negation. It sets before it no aims that are to be realised in the world, but is simply the most profound effort to attain to the state of keeping completely pure from the world.

But Gandhi places Ahimsā at the service of world and life affirmation directed to activity in the world. With him Ahimsā engages in activity within the world and in this way it ceases to be what in essence it is.

Passive resistance is a non-violent use of force. The idea is that by circumstances brought about without violence pressure is brought to bear on the opponent and he is forced to yield. Being an attack that is more difficult to parry than an active attack, passive resistance may be the more successful method. But there is also a danger that this concealed application of force may cause more bitterness than an open use of violence. In any case the difference between passive and active resistance is only quite relative.

When Gandhi enlists Ahimsā in the service of passive resistance he unites the non-worldly and the worldly. He has not been spared the painful experience that in such circumstances the worldly may prove stronger than the non-worldly.

One can even question whether this has not often been the case with himself. Most often he has applied the principle of passive resistance without leaving his opponent the necessary time to come to meet him half-way. There is in his character a vehemence which prevents him from patiently letting his confidence rest in the purely spiritual operation of an idea. He has never succeeded in altogether controlling the agitator within his breast.

He is confident that by the non-worldly he can completely spiritualise and ennoble what is worldly, and he really seriously believes that he can practise passive resistance entirely in the spirit of freedom from hatred and of love. Again and again he points out to his followers that the justification, the reason and the success of what they join him in undertaking for the good of the people is dependent on whether their minds are completely purified. And again and again he emphasises his conviction that passive resistance, exercised in the spirit of Ahiṃsā, must not only be concerned with the achievement of this purpose or that, but that its real aim must be to bring about a mutual understanding founded on love. The non-violent violence of passive resistance must merely form the river-bed for the flood-waters of the spirit of love.

Thus, then, does Gandhi try to solve the problem whether, along with action by ethical and spiritual means, action by worldly means can also be justified. —he sets up the first as a principle and at the same time retains a minimum of worldly procedure, the exercise, namely, of non-violent force ; and this he places at the service of the ethical and the spiritual.

It must remain a question whether the restriction to non-violent force and the combination of this (as being the procedure regarded as the least worldly) with the ethical and spiritual method is the right solution of the problem. All mixing up of what is different in essence is an unnatural and dangerous proceeding.

There can also come under consideration a solution which refuses such a limitation of the use of force and in this way upholds the separation between the worldly and the ethical and spiritual. The method is as follows. In combination with the ethical and spiritual means, recourse will be had to worldly purposive procedure. But when the use of force seems unavoidable, then as little force as possible will be employed. And it will be used in such a way that it is regarded only as a last expedient, and will be exercised, not in a worldly, but in an ethical spirit. The important thing is not that only non-violent force should be employed, but that all worldly purposive action should be undertaken with the greatest possible avoidance of violence, and that ethical considerations should so dominate ourselves as to influence also the hearts of our opponents. In as far as possible restricting worldly procedure; in explaining and justifying it; in making it effective in the right way, through the ethical disposition which lies behind it: in *such* an application of force in the spirit of non-violence lies the solution of the problem. But even if one doubts whether Gandhi's method is right in itself and whether the way he has carried out his experiment can give satisfaction, one must nevertheless recognise his extraordinary service in having opened up the problem of activity and pointed to the profound truth that only activity in an ethical spirit can really accomplish anything.

The fact that Gandhi has united the idea of Ahimsā to the idea of activity directed on the world has the importance not merely of an event in the thought of India but in that of humanity. Through him the attention of ethics is again directed to a fact which had been too much neglected: namely, that the use of force does not become ethically permissible because it has an ethical aim, but that in addition it must be applied in a completely ethical disposition.

In a conversation with his friend, the Rev. J. J. Doke, a Baptist minister of Johannesburg, Gandhi said that he got the idea of passive resistance in the spirit of Ahimsā from the sayings of Jesus, " But I say unto you, that ye resist not evil ", and " Love your enemies . . . pray for them which despitefully use you and persecute you ; that ye may be the children of your Father which is in heaven ". And then his idea developed under the influence of the Bhagavad-Gītā and Tolstoi's " The Kingdom of God is Within You ".

It is hard to explain the fact that Gandhi's attitude to war is not completely determined by Ahismā. That he served in the Boer War as a volunteer in the Ambulance Corps and would have done the same in the Great War, if he had not been compelled by his health to give up the project, can be understood by his anxiety to alleviate the misery of war ; but that in India he tried to enlist volunteers for service as combatants is absolutely irreconcilable with Ahimsā. He allowed himself to be led astray by the consideration that by such help given in her time of need England might be induced to recognise the rights of the Indian People. But Ahimsā is a principle high uplifted above all politics.

And from the standpoint of Ahimsā it is strange that Gandhi regards it as so important that his people should retain the right to arm themselves.

Great as is his interest in reality, world and life negation nevertheless plays a part in his mode of thought.

He is concerned with the welfare of the people, but at the same time he disavows the ideal of achieving national prosperity. He wishes property to be restricted to what is absolutely necessary for the maintenance of life. Even those who have the means shall not allow themselves to lead a life adjusted to higher pretensions. Through this ideal of the smallest possible needs and smallest possible possessions Gandhi expects that civilisation will be cured of its ills. The fact that he is in agreement with Tolstoi about this is to him a proof that he is championing the right.

World and life negation is very strongly expressed in his *Confession of Faith* (1909) which treats of true civilisation. In this he adjudges to quack medicine a superiority over modern medical science. "The salvation of India", so runs one passage, "lies in its forgetting all it has learnt during the last fifty years. Railways, telegraphs, hospitals, lawyers, doctors and the rest must one and all disappear, and the so-called upper classes must learn conscientiously, piously and thoughtfully to lead the life of the simple peasant because they recognise that this is the life that bestows real happiness upon us."

Later, in prison, while suffering the tortures of appendicitis, he resolved to accept the aid which the modern scientific art of healing he had so severely condemned could bring him. He allowed an operation to be performed. But he cannot get rid of the thought that in this he acted contrary to his real conviction. "I admit", he wrote in a letter to a Brahmin ascetic who had taken him to task about this apostasy, "that it was a weakness of soul to submit to the surgical operation. Had I been altogether free from self-seeking, I should have resigned myself to the inevitable; but I was mastered by the wish to go on living in this body of mine."

Of late he has nevertheless allowed that modern medicine and modern hospitals may be in some measure justified.

His world and life negation comes to full expression when he not only demands the taming of the desires but sets up the ideal of celibacy.

He knows from experience the misery of child-marriage. His family brought about his marriage when he was thirteen years of age. His wife has proved a faithful and patient life-companion. Four sons were born of the marriage.

Gandhi supports celibacy on two grounds. The first is his view that only the man who has renounced all desires possesses the spirituality necessary for true activity. He wrote once, " Whoever wishes to dedicate himself to the service of his country or to perceive something of the glory of the truly religious life, must lead a life of chastity, whether he be married or unmarried ". The second reason lies in his belief in reincarnation. To a question as to his attitude to marriage, he replied, " The goal of life is redemption. As a Hindu I believe that this redemption—we call it Moksa—consists in deliverance from re-birth ; it is then that we burst the fetters of the flesh, it is then that we become one with God. Now marriage is a hindrance on the way to the highest goal in so far namely as it draws the bonds of the flesh still tighter. Celibacy on the other hand is a powerful aid, for it makes it possible for us to lead a life of complete devotion to God."

But in spite of this strong world and life negation, Gandhi can no longer make his own the old ideal which is part and parcel of it—the ideal of a life withdrawn from the world. His friend the Brahmin ascetic, who advised him to retire to a cave and live for meditation alone, received the reply, " I am striving to reach the Kingdom of Heaven which is called the liberation of the soul. In order to reach this I need not seek refuge in a cave. I carry my cave with me. . . ."

By a magnificent paradox Gandhi brings the idea of activity and the idea of world and life negation into relationship in such a way that he can regard activity in the world as the highest form of renunciation of the world. In a letter to the Brahmin ascetic, he says, " My service to my people is part of the discipline to which I subject myself in order to free my soul from the bonds of the flesh. . . . For me the path to salvation leads through unceasing tribulation in the service of my fellow-countrymen and humanity."

So in Gandhi's spirit modern Indian ethical world and life affirmation and a world and life negation which goes back to the Buddha dwell side by side.

* *
*

Modern Indian thought makes a noble attempt to get really clear about itself in Rabīndranāth Tagore, the son of Debendranāth Tagore.

Rabīndranāth Tagore (b. 1861) is at the same time thinker, poet and musician. He has himself translated his important works into English. The attention of Europe was directed to him by his becoming the recipient of the Nobel Prize for Literature in 1913. For many years he has lived at Santiniketan in Bengal, where since 1921 he has built up a school and college on modern educational lines.

His world view is found most clearly expressed in his book *Sādhanā* (English edition 1913, German 1921). It contains lectures delivered at Harvard University. Sādhanā means " attainment ", in a figurative sense " fulfilment ".

With Tagore it is no longer a question of world and life negation making larger or smaller concessions to world and life affirmation. Ethical world and life affirmation has completely triumphed. It governs his world-view and will suffer nothing of world and life negation beside it.

Tagore recognises also that thought must decide either for world and life negation or for world and life affirmation. For the sake of ethics he decisively declares himself in favour of world and life affirmation. This has all the significance of a really great deed. A process of development which has been going on for centuries reaches in him its natural conclusion.

Tagore calls it an aberration of oriental thought that though it is occupied only with the question of union with God, yet it does not permit man to reach a positive relationship to the world which proceeded from God. He has some hard words for the Sannyāsins (ascetics) who devote themselves to renunciation of the world. Similarly, however, he condemns the European who has lost inwardness and whose activity in the world no longer results from spiritual self-surrender to God. He demands both things together: that man should belong to God with his soul and serve Him actively in His world.

Joy in life and joy in creation belong, according to Tagore, to the nature of man. We cannot, he argues, rest content with only accomplishing what conduces to the preservation and enjoyment of our life, but if our humanity is not stunted we also have in us the impulse to act in harmony with the World Spirit and lend a hand in perfecting the Universe.

" Of course it is obvious that the world serves us and fulfils our needs, but our relation to it does not end there. We are bound to it with a deeper and truer bond than that of necessity. Our soul is drawn to it; our love of life is really our wish to continue our relation with this great world. This relation is one of love" (*Sādhanā*, ch. v. p. 112).

Because of the mysterious interest he takes in the

world, man constantly seeks to enlarge the domain of his knowledge and power. He wishes that the blessings of well-being shall fall to the lot of all; that wisdom and justice shall reign; that relief shall be found for pain and suffering; that art and poetry shall be developed and shall ennoble men's minds, and that the mysterious forces of Nature shall be made serviceable in realising for us illimitable progress.

Mankind, then, is to attain to true civilisation. But true civilisation, according to Tagore, is only present where rules the profoundest and noblest spirit of humanity. Material achievements are something that is relative. They only end in blessing for us when mankind also makes progress in matters spiritual and ethical.

"Civilisation must be judged and prized, not by the amount of power it has developed, but by how much it has evolved and given expression to, by its laws and institutions, the love of humanity" (*Sādhanā*, ch. v. p. 111).

So Tagore represents an ethical world and life affirmation governed by the ideal of true humanity to which—though he fails to establish this fact—the noblest thinkers of the West, a Shaftesbury (1671–1713), a Kant (1724–1804) and a Fichte (1762–1814) have professed adherence before him.

For in European thought, although by its very nature it is in danger of not sufficiently keeping men on the path of inwardness, and has altogether too much neglected this aspect of life, there may yet be discerned profound and heartfelt world and life affirmation.

* *
*

It is a weakness in Tagore that he tries to proclaim his world and life affirming ethical mysticism as ancient Indian wisdom. He will not admit that Indian thought has gone through a process of development.

To justify his arbitrary interpretation of the ancient texts, he lays down the theory that we are not concerned at all with determining their original meaning. All that matters is to recognise the meaning they have for *us* and to show forth in our lives the truth we find in them for ourselves.

" This is the reason why the teachings of our greatest prophets give rise to endless disputations when we try to understand them by following their words and not by realising them in our own lives. The men who are cursed with the gift of the literal mind are the unfortunate ones who are always busy with their nets and neglect the fishing " (*Sādhanā*, ch. iv. p. 72).

But, to continue Tagore's metaphor, those who have not the literal mind fish with nets that are ill cared for and full of holes, and that too is wrong.

By the people who are cursed with the gift of the literal mind Tagore means the European scholars who busy themselves with critical scientific investigations in order to define the original meaning of the Vedic writings and to make clear the difference between the ancient Brahmin supra-ethical world and life negation and the neo-Indian ethical mysticism of union with God.

That we ought to determine and accept the original literal meaning of the Vedic texts is a principle which we dare not override. Even historical Truth is Truth, and must be respected as such. Thought must be absolutely independent and fearless.

Tagore gets the evidence that his ethical world and

life affirmation is contained in the Vedic writings by setting forth certain world and life affirming sentences of the Upanishads in such a way that they describe God as the loving Creator of a Universe filled with wonderful harmony and tell of the joyous self-devotion of man to Him and to His work. He does not allow their due to the powerful passages of the Upanishads which describe the Brahman as pure Being without any qualities and treat of union with Him in renunciation of the world and in non-activity.

Tagore is in the right when he draws our attention to the presence of world and life affirmation in the Upanishads and right too in the value he lays upon it. We Europeans have inherited from Schopenhauer and Deussen a tendency to give too little attention to the ideas of world and life affirmation which are found in the Upanishads. It is a fact that world and life negation and world and life affirmation are found side by side in the Upanishads. But—and the critical scientific scholars are clearer about this than is Tagore—world and life negation in the Upanishads is the newly discovered great truth which overshadows world and life affirmation.

In the construction of an ideal of living for the Brahmin, world and life negation makes far-reaching concessions to world and life affirmation. But it retains its predominance in thought, and in theory it is the current truth.

We must also consider the relationship in which the world and life affirmation expressed in the Upanishads stands to ethics. We find there an ethic which is concerned only with the virtues and duties enforced by the authority of tradition. The Upanishads have not got so far as to know of an ethic based on thought and therefore know nothing either of the union of such an ethic with world and life affirmation as it is effected in the thought of Tagore. Certainly Tagore can point in the Upanishads to world and life affirmation and ethics existing side by side. But this is not his own profound ethical world and life affirmation which he possesses in common with the noblest thinkers of modern Europe. That only came into being after a long process of historical development.

If the ethical world and life affirmation which Tagore thinks he finds in the Upanishads had really been contained in them, a Will to ethical progress must have resulted from it in the very period of the Upanishads, and this Will could not have done otherwise than demand social reforms. That the spirit of India through long centuries merely accepted the most terrible abuses as appertaining to this world and has only in modern times attempted to create better conditions proves that there was not yet present in the Upanishads—though single phrases may be interpreted in this sense—that ethical world and life affirmation founded on thought which bids man engage in personal idealistic activity in the world.

Truth requires no other authority than that which it contains within itself. If the witness of the past can be brought forward to support it, it more easily finds recognition and more easily gains currency than without that witness. But a truth must never be violently interpolated into the thought of an earlier period in order that it may there find justification. In itself Truth possesses such power of carrying conviction that it has no need to turn to History to beg for a recommendation.

When he attempts to give a solid foundation to the world-view of ethical world and life affirmation, Tagore, like the Western thinkers who undertake a similar task, is faced by the three great problems: (1) how the Primal Cause of Being can be regarded as an ethical personality; (2) in how far the Universe and what happens in it can be explained as ethical and fraught with meaning; (3) in how far human activity in union with the creative Spirit of the Universe is conceivable.

Tagore does not take into account the difficulty of thinking of the Primal Cause of Being as also a personality, let alone an ethical personality. With magnificent ingenuousness he simultaneously identifies God with the Universe and regards Him as its Creator. It matters nothing to him that he is thinking on dualistic lines if he speaks even once only of God as the Creator of the world. He wanders to and fro between monism and dualism as if there were no gulf between them.

What is great about the Brahmins is that they do not apply the conception of God which had its rise in the popular religion to the Primal Cause of Being. But Tagore does so without feeling the need of justifying himself on this score. Just as if he were not the descendant of Brahmins, he mixes up belief and thought just as Europeans did for so long.

He does not even pay the attention it demands to the difficulty of attributing an ethical character to the Primal Cause.

In order to be able to regard the Universe as

having a meaning—here again just as we Europeans used to do—he interprets it in such a way as to attribute meaning to it. And to do this he actually goes back to the ancient Brahmanic idea that the sensuous world is a play which God stages for Himself. For the Brahmins—and even as late as the Bhagavad-Gītā—this play consists in a series of events which cannot be further explained. But Tagore, because he stands for ethical world and life affirmation, is obliged, like Fichte, to seek to understand the play as the profoundest expression of the divine nature. God, he explains, makes the Universe proceed from Himself because His nature is love. Love can only realise itself in the fusion of two individualities. So God must have beside Him something which possesses a certain independence in its relation to Him.

"Not only in our self but also in nature is there this separateness from God, which has been described as *māyā* by our philosophers, because the separateness does not exist by itself, it does not limit God's infinity from outside. It is his own will that has imposed limits to itself, just as the chess-player restricts his will with regard to the moving of the chessmen. The player willingly enters into definite relations with each particular piece and realises the joy of his power by these very restrictions. It is not that he cannot move the chessmen just as he pleases, but if he does so then there can be no play. If God assumes his rôle of omnipotence, then his creation is at an end and his power loses all its meaning. For power to be a power must act within limits" (*Sādhanā*, ch. iv. p. 86).

"As by the limits of law nature is separated from God, so it is the limits of its egoism which separate the self from him. He has willingly set limits to his will, and has given us mastery over the little world of our own. . . . The reason of it is that the will, which is love's will and therefore free, can have its joy only in a union with another free will" (*Sādhanā*, ch. iv. pp. 86, 87).

Thus this play of love (*līlā*) between God and the human soul goes on unceasingly for ever and ever. If the soul realises that it is the bride of the Lord of the Universe, it knows also that the Universe is its own home. "Then all her services become services of love, all the troubles and tribulations of life come to her as trials triumphantly borne to prove the strength of her love, smilingly to win the wager from her lover" (*Sādhanā*, ch. viii. p. 161).

Similar thoughts are found in Western mystics inspired by the Song of Solomon.

So the Brahmanic explanation of the Universe as a play, which originated in world and life negation, is transferred by Tagore to world and life affirmation and there receives quite a new significance.

In Tagore's belief, as in that of the Western representatives of ethical world and life affirmation, the infinite Universe was created for man. That man should be united to God in love is regarded as the fulfilment of the meaning of the Universe.

Tagore cannot admit that human thought must accept the Universe as something inexplicable. Like the European rationalists of the 18th century he tries to interpret it optimistically and maintains that it is governed by beauty, harmony and order. What we observe in the world of ugliness, disharmony, disorder and sorrow is intended, he explains, to dissolve into beauty, harmony, order and joy. All misfortune that befalls a man, if he knows the right way of meeting it, ends in happiness.

"Through our sense of truth we realise law in creation, and through our sense of beauty we realise harmony in the Universe" (*Sādhanā*, ch. vii. p. 141).

We think we are listening to Shaftesbury.

According to Tagore no kind of pessimistic view has any justification. He regards pessimism as a pose of brain and heart.

He takes as little account of the difficulties of the problem of action for furthering the purposes of the Spirit of the Universe as does Fichte. He simply assumes that all action in which man gets beyond his little *ego* serves towards the realisation of the world-purpose. The world-will, he says, is for us no alien thing. We experience it in ourselves. All that matters is that we should completely surrender ourselves to it. In a certain sense the world must become our larger body and our *ego* must expand into the world-*ego*.

The French philosophers Alfred Fouillée (1838–1913) and Jean Marie Guyau (1854–1888) also talk of a similar expansion of the *ego*. But by this they understand only that man feels himself so united ethically to other beings that he experiences their fate as if it were his own and is as much concerned for them as for himself.

With Tagore it is not merely a question of the ethical expansion of the *ego*, but also of an expansion which results from the increased capacity for action.

" Thus, through the help of science, as we come to know more of the laws of nature, we gain in power; we tend to attain a universal body. Our organ of sight, our organ of locomotion, our physical strength becomes world-wide; steam and electricity become our nerve and muscle. . . . And in this age of science it is our endeavour fully to establish our claim to our world-self. . . . Really, there is no limit to our powers, for we are not outside the universal power which is the expression of universal law " (*Sādhanā*, ch. iii. pp. 61, 62).

In the exercise as an ethical personality of activity in correspondence with every form of his capacity, man, according to Tagore, experiences union with God in love. In his own person he realises Him who is the highest Self. His love is united to the eternal Love.

" All that we can ever strive after is to become ever more one with God ".

Tagore sets up the true ideal of ethical world-view when in similar fashion he demands spiritual as well as active union with infinite Being and derives activity from spiritual sources. But he cannot succeed in basing this world-view on real knowledge of the Universe. He derives it from an optimistic-ethical interpretation of the world which is related to that of Shaftesbury and Fichte and is as little capable of satisfying critical thought as theirs is.

When Indian thought takes ethical world and life affirmation seriously, it finds itself—as we see in Tagore—facing the same problems, and finally attempting the same solutions, as the thought of Europe.

In Tagore's magnificent thought-symphony the harmonies and modulations are Indian. But the themes remind us of those of European thought.

His doctrine of Soul-in-all-things is no longer that of the Upanishads, but that of a mode of thought under the influence of modern natural science.

Tagore has not yet studied the question whether ethical idealism must not renounce—and whether it can renounce—the claim that its foundations rest on knowledge of the Universe. It is a thought which, for him, still lies quite beyond the horizon.

So he is as little able as the others who had

attempted it before him really to found the world-view of ethical world and life affirmation on knowledge of the Universe. But the Goethe of India gives expression to his personal experience that this is the truth in a manner more profound, more powerful and more charming than any man has ever done before him. This completely noble and harmonious thinker belongs not only to his own people but to humanity.

Aurobindo Ghose (b. 1872), like Tagore, attempts to explain Brahmanic mysticism in the sense of ethical world and life affirmation. In earlier years he felt himself called to political activity for the liberation of India from British rule, but in the year 1910 he withdrew, as Tagore had already done, from politics, and since then has lived in Pondicherry solely occupied with the renewal of Indian thought. He wants to lead his countrymen out of the temples and out of the narrowness of the schools of learning into life itself. " The past ", he says, " must be sacred to us, but the future still more sacred ". He is as firmly convinced as Vivekānanda that the spirit of India is destined to lead mankind, while Tagore sets his hopes on a philosophy in which the thought of the East and the thought of the West will unite in sharing what is best and most profound in each other's spiritual possessions.

It is too soon to judge in how far the latest Indian philosophy, which is represented by a number of men of remarkable talent, is really free and creative, and in how far it grasps the full import of the problems it has to face.

S. Radhakrishnan (b. 1888) is strongly influenced by Tagore.

CHAPTER XVI

LOOKING BACKWARD AND FORWARD

AS a valuable gift from the magical mysticism which was its starting-point, Indian thought received the perception that world-view is mysticism, that is to say the spiritual union of man with infinite Being. What is great about it is that it holds fast to this belief unswervingly.

But from magical mysticism it also derived world and life negation.

In the hands of the Brahmins it dropped out of the natural key of world and life affirmation into the unnatural key of world and life negation. It could not, however, continue in this key permanently, but, constrained by ethics, had to modulate back into the original key of world and life affirmation.

Thus the development of Indian thought was determined by a conflict between world and life negation and world and life affirmation. But this warfare between giants went on in secrecy and in silence. The two views did not make their appearance by an open opposition of fundamental principles, but the issue was decided by world and life negation making ever greater concessions to world and life affirmation, which more and more prevailed over the world and life negation which had been maintained as long as possible as a fundamental principle.

Even the Brahmins of antiquity made to world and life affirmation the great concession that it was only during the second half of their lives that they began actually to practise world and life negation.

World and life denial is to a very great extent qualified when the Buddha falls away from strict asceticism and makes a general demand for inner freedom from the world rather than for outward denial of the world practised in detail. And in his ethics we already find the idea of action. But the Buddha does not venture so far as to attack world and life negation from the standpoint of ethics.

In the Bhagavad-Gītā action and abstention from action are recognised as equally justified. Indeed action is placed even higher than refraining from action. But this is based in such a way on the idea of self-devotion to God that world and life negation, although as a matter of fact it loses its validity, is not in principle denied.

In proportion as ethics are developed and gain significance in Indian thought, and in proportion as the justification of action is directly based on ethical necessity, so it becomes impossible for world and life negation still to be maintained even in theory. If ethics, as they must, proceed in a spirit of love to engage in action aimed at the creation of better conditions in the world, they thereupon enter into open opposition to world and life denial.

What happens in Indian thought confirms the result of pure reflection: namely, that the world-view of world and life negation has not equal justification with that of world and life affirmation and cannot enter into competition with it. By its very nature it is impracticable. In measure as it becomes ethical, it ceases to exist.

*   *

*

Western and Indian thought are both, each in its

own way, incomplete and do not go far enough. If one wants to give each its due, one must not only look to their fundamental difference, but must also take into consideration the fact that both are undergoing change.

The change began simultaneously in both, about the middle of the 19th century.

In European thought the change consists in being unable to maintain the truth of the world-knowledge on which it has hitherto rested, and having now to attempt to establish the world-view of ethical world and life affirmation by processes of thought that are absolutely conditioned by reality. For Indian thought the task is to give up world and life negation and adjust itself to ethical world and life affirmation.

Western thought was capable of representing the highest ideals so long as it was unsophisticated enough to regard its interpretation of the world in the sense of ethical world and life affirmation as knowledge of the Universe. The reproach that it fails to confer on mankind sufficient inwardness and spirituality really applies only to present-day, and not to earlier, thought. In the men of the 18th and even of the beginning of the 19th century the idea of action is found united with splendid spirituality and inwardness. The fact that European thinking is not mystical but doctrinaire had then scarcely made itself felt. By its explanation of the Universe it brought man into spiritual relationship with infinite Being. But when it was forced to abandon that explanation, then it not only became a question how it could give to the convictions of man a foundation derived from his spiritual relationship to infinite Being, but there was also a danger of its renouncing the hope of exploring this problem at all.

In the middle of the 19th century the explanation of the Universe offered by speculative philosophy, and that drawn from ethical world and life affirmation in general both completely collapsed. The systems of Fichte, Schelling and Hegel were last attempts to uphold something of that explanation. Thenceforth Western thought had to resign itself to a discussion of reality. But it could not succeed in basing ideals of ethical world and life affirmation upon a reality which could be neither interpreted nor idealised, and thus it came to abandon part of its position. It represents a world and life affirmation which is no longer completely ethical. Instead of retaining the ideals which correspond to the profoundest ethical world and life affirmation and undertaking to re-shape reality in accordance with them, it endeavours now to derive ideals from reality. And it reaches a point where it no longer allows man to be preoccupied with his relation to infinite Being, but only with his relation to human society.

This is what is so petty and so thoroughly in accordance with the spirit of the age in the philosophy of Nietzsche, namely that it is really only concerned with man and society and knows nothing of the problem of man and the Universe. In this philosophy the Universe is a mere stage-setting.

Western thought is not governed like mystical thought by the idea that the one thing needful is the spiritual union of man with infinite Being, and therefore (if it is obliged to renounce the hope of attaining to a knowledge of the Universe that corresponds to ethical world and life affirmation), it is in danger of saying it is satisfied not only with lowered ideals, but also with an inferior conception of world-view. That is the tragedy that is being enacted before our eyes.

*   *
*

It is easy to understand that Indian thought feels superior to this mode of thinking which has fallen into confusion and suffered damage in its struggle with reality. But if it believes itself superior to Western thought as such, this only proves that it is insufficiently acquainted with that thought and does not rightly appreciate its practical achievements.

Vivekānanda and others are willing and glad to concede to European thought that it has the capacity for making scientific discoveries, for creating machines, for organising the life of society in an expedient fashion, and in general for accomplishing the work of civilisation. But in their utterances they take it as a matter of course that Indian thought is far superior in its achievements so far as thinking is concerned. Vivekānanda wants " to revolutionise the world " with the eternal verities which are in the possession of India. According to a saying of Aurobindo Ghose, India holds in its hand the key to the progress of humanity.

Vivekānanda and the rest believe the world must accept mysticism from India. They do not take into consideration that in Western thought there is mysticism of a similar nature to and no less valuable than the mysticism in Indian thought. They work with the fiction that Indian thought alone is capable of profundity and piety. They do not understand that mysticism only fails to make headway in European thought because it cannot comply with the demands of ethical world and life affirmation.

It cannot remain hidden from Indian thinkers that their own mysticism is in this respect still less satisfying. From time to time Vivekānanda expresses himself quite despairingly to the effect that the West can point to such great social achievements, whilst in India, the home of the eternal verities, so little is done for the poor and the suffering. On one occasion he confesses, " No society puts its foot on the neck of the wretched so mercilessly as does that of India ". In one of his letters to Indian friends one finds the sentence, " So far as the spiritual and mental qualities are concerned, the Americans are greatly our inferiors, but as a social community they are superior to us ".

Vivekānanda dares not probe to its depths the question why Indian mentality is so poor in works. He puts the responsibility on the indifference of individuals. He will not admit to himself that the guilt lies with a mode of thinking which involves withdrawal from the world. He cannot concede indeed that Indian thought has undergone any development and that the idea of active love has only begun to play a part within it in recent times.

* * *

Indian thought is only at the beginning of the change which it has to go through. The simple recognition of ethical world and life affirmation is not enough. The new cannot be simply dovetailed into the old. It is of the nature of leaven.

World and life negation enables Indian thought to avoid trying conclusions with reality. But world and life affirmation involves a compulsion to relate everything to the facts of reality. It will work itself out in Indian in the same way as in European thought. Indian thought will not be able to preserve the ingenuousness it still possesses, but through world and life affirmation it will be led on to the path of realism which Western thought was forced to tread.

The thought of India to-day is that of a period of transition. In the period which is approaching it must find enough insight and courage to examine itself and to shake off what cannot be reconciled with the spirit of reality. In its knowledge of the Suprasensuous it must determine to keep within the bounds set to our power of perception, must determine to renounce the aid of fantasy and poetry on which it has drawn so plenteously up to the present, to give up the elastic conception of truth of which it has hitherto availed itself and determine finally to make itself independent of the authority of tradition.

We await the Indian thinker who will expound to us the mysticism of spiritual union with infinite Being as it is in itself, not as it is set down in the ancient texts or according to the meaning read into them by their interpreters.

It belongs to the nature of mysticism that it is timeless and appeals to no other authority than that of the truth which it carries within it.

The pathway from imperfect to perfect recognised

Thought in Terms of Reality and Mysticism

truth leads through the valley of reality. European thought has already descended into this valley. Indian thought is still on the hill on this side of it. If it wishes to climb to the hill beyond, it must first go down into the valley.

Because the thought of India is still unsophisticated, it is still self-conscious and busied with its mission to the world. The deepest thinking is humble. It is only concerned that the flame of truth which it keeps alive should burn with the strongest and purest heat; it does not trouble about the distance to which its brightness penetrates.

* * *

So Western and Indian thought face together the task of finding for the mysticism of ethical world and life affirmation foundations that are based on what accords with reality.

If thought, in so far as it has attempted it, has not been able to solve this problem, the explanation is that it has laboured under the mistake that world-view can and must be founded on knowledge of the Universe.

But we possess no knowledge of the Universe which can point us to a world-purpose at whose service we have to place our ethical activity. It was because thought believed it could not get on without knowledge of the Universe that it created such knowledge for itself by its interpretation of the Universe.

The dualistic world-views contain an interpretation of the world in the sense of ethical world and life affirmation, but such interpretation, though it may be more obscure, is also found in mysticism when it has any kind of ethical and world and life affirming character.

The mysticism which denies the world and life has no need of an explanation of the Universe. It is contented with establishing the fact that the only sensible course of action which men have to take into account is to reflect on their identity with the Spirit of the Universe. But as soon as mysticism stands for the thought that man has to realise spiritual unity with eternal Being in action as well, it must correspondingly advance towards an explanation of the Universe. Now it sees itself compelled in some way or other to adopt the thought that the World-Spirit is creative Will and can therefore only attain to consciousness of itself in men who engage in action in conformity with the World-Will.

But this explanation cannot be sustained because the World-Will remains to us an enigma. Wherever it is put forward, in the Bhagavad-Gītā, in Fichte, in Tagore and the rest, it ends in saying that man has to take part in the drama of action which the World-Spirit stages for Itself. But it is impossible to make this drama and participation in it comprehensible as being fraught with meaning and ethical. For by its very nature a play can neither be full of meaning nor ethical. It treats merely of fantasies of thought which only represent something because of the magnificent words in which they are clothed. Reduced to their simplest terms, they are absolutely unsatisfying.

So the mysticism of world and life affirmation, like

that of world and life negation, is obliged to renounce knowledge of the Universe.

* * *

But how can man become one with the World-Spirit in action when he confesses to himself that both the nature and the aim of its creative activity remain for him a secret?

The activity of the World-Spirit is a riddle to us because it runs its course in creation and in devastation, in bringing forth and in destroying life. What happens in Nature therefore cannot enable us to deduce the principle for an activity by which we can step out of an existence for ourselves alone in order to influence the world in the sense of the World-Spirit. So that for us there can really be no question of activity in co-operation with the Spirit of the Universe, but only of devoting ourselves to an activity through which we may experience spiritual union with that Spirit. Only when thought has recognised this fact does it finally free itself from the endeavour to base world-view openly or covertly on knowledge of the Universe.

We feel that the activity by which we become one with the Spirit of the Universe is ethical activity. How can we understand this?

Only a complete ethic has mystical significance. An ethical system which is only concerned with the attitude of man to his fellow-man and to society cannot really be in harmony with a world-view. It has no relationship with the Universe. To found an ethical world-view on ethics which are only concerned with our fellow-man and human society is a logical impossibility. It is the fault of too narrow a conception of ethics that thought has so far been unable to present an ethical world-view in a way that carries conviction.

Only when ethics embrace the whole Universe is an ethical world-view really possible. And then only does it become apparent that the ethical world-view is ethical mysticism.

True ethics are world-wide. All that is ethical goes back to a single principle of morality, namely the maintenance of life at its highest level, and the furtherance of life. The maintenance of one's own life at the highest level by becoming more and more perfect in spirit, and the maintenance at the highest level of other life by sympathetic, helpful self-devotion to it—this is ethics. What we call love is in its essence reverence for life. All material and spiritual values are values only in so far as they serve the maintenance of life at its highest level and the furtherance of life.

Ethics are boundless in their domain and limitless in their demands. They are concerned with all living things that come within our sphere.

In the recognition and manifestation in action of our connection with all existences, we become united in active fashion, and in the only possible way open to us, with infinite Being. Our self-devotion to life with a view to furthering it and maintaining it at its highest value constitutes active union with the eternal Being, completing the union in thought which consists in resignation to what happens in the Universe.

Our activity is only directed to the Infinite if it is actively governed by ethics that are absolute and know no limits. Only under the guidance of such ethics is our activity comprehensible as giving effect to the experience of spiritual union with infinite Being and a constant renewal of that experience.

A true and valuable world-view does not come from knowledge of the Universe, but from knowledge of the nature and range of ethics.

* *
*

The ethical determination of our will to live goes back to the physical fact that our life has sprung from other life and allows other life to proceed from it. So we cannot rest in a complete state of existence for ourselves alone, and we refuse to rest in it because of our close relationship with the life from which we derive and with that derived from ourselves. Thus the most rudimentary ethics as found not only in mankind but in the more highly developed animals are a giving effect in action to the solidarity with other life which is directly related to us.

But if thought once begins to occupy itself with the mysterious fact of ethics, it cannot succeed in defining the limits of solidarity with other life. It must widen the circle from the narrowest limits of the family first to include the clan, then the tribe, then the nation and finally all mankind. But even when it has established the relationship between man and every other man it cannot stop. By reason of the quite universal idea, which is as elastic as one pleases, of participation in a common nature, it is compelled to declare the unity of mankind with all created beings.

The ethic that knows no limits has in common with the Upanishads the knowledge of the *Tat twam asi*—that man "must see himself in all beings and see all beings in himself".[1] But whereas for ethics this knowledge is established in a direct way and as a motive for action, in the Upanishads it is deduced from the doctrine that the universal Soul is in all individual souls, and therefore it has no ethical, but only a theoretical, significance.

Ethics consist in responsibility towards all that lives—responsibility which has become so wide as to be limitless.

Action directed towards the world is only possible for man in so far as he strives for the maintenance and furtherance at its highest level of all life that comes within his range. In this becoming-one with all life he realises the active becoming-one with the Primal Source of Being to which this life belongs.

* *
*

There are two kinds of mysticism: the one kind resulting from the assumption that the World-Spirit and the spirit of man are identical, and the other of ethical origin.

The mysticism of identity, whether Indian or European, is not ethical either in origin or in nature and cannot become so. Ethical thoughts can only be found in it and developed from it in so far as an ethical nature is attributed to the World-Spirit. But as soon as thinking even in the very least degree leaves the position that the World-Spirit and world

---

[1] See pp. 36 and 43.

events are an unfathomable secret, that thinking is no longer in harmony with reality.

In measure as the ethical element in Indian thought develops and gains recognition, so does that thought see itself compelled to attempt the impossible task of comprehending its mysticism of identity as ethical. But it can no more succeed than did Master Eckhart succeed in making his mysticism become ethical. The attempt invariably consists in nothing more than adding an ethical element to mysticism by means of inadmissible explanations.

The mysticism which derives from ethics on the other hand is completely in touch with reality. It can reconcile itself to the fact that the World-Spirit and world events remain to us incomprehensible. Since it need not make trial of any kind of explanation of the Universe, it engages in no conflict with the knowledge gained by experience. Whilst the other mysticism regards this knowledge with contempt and appeals in face of it to an intuitive knowledge of the Universe, this ethical mysticism recognises the importance of that knowledge. It knows that all knowledge grounded in experience only leads deeper and deeper into the great mystery that all that is is Will-to-Live.

Ethical mysticism is completely in earnest about the " knowing ignorance " (*docta ignorantia*) talked of by mediaeval mystics. Only for ethical mysticism this is not, as for the other mysticism, something alongside and above the knowledge drawn from experience, but is what results from that knowledge.

The enlightened ignorance of ethical mysticism is ignorance in so far as it admits how absolutely mysterious and unfathomable are the world and life. It is knowledge in so far as it does know the one thing which we can and must know in the sphere of this mystery, namely, that all Being is Life, and that in loving self-devotion to other life we realise our spiritual union with infinite Being.

Ethical mysticism humbly leaves unanswered the question in what manner the World-Spirit exists within the poor human spirit and in it attains to consciousness of itself. It holds only to the fact that the poor human spirit, by leaving behind its existence for itself alone, in the devotion of service to other life experiences union with the World-Spirit and thereby becomes enriched and finds peace.

In the mysticism derived from ethics man possesses directly and inalienably a world-view in which all the ideals of true humanity are firmly grounded, and from this at the same time he draws the most profound spirituality and the strongest incentive to activity.

The fact that the world-view of ethical world and life affirmation must be based, not on knowledge of the Universe, but on ethics, began to be realised even in the 18th century. In Kant it is already so far established that he tries to prove his world-view by premisses which go beyond the knowledge gained by experience, namely by ethics, as being the fundamental fact of spiritual and mental life. Thought arrives at the end of the path pointed by the recognition of this truth, if it understands ethics as self-devotion to all life, and if it recognises that the mysticism which results from limitless ethics contains in itself a world-view of ethical world and life affirmation which is independent of all knowledge of the Universe.

The more ethical Indian thought becomes, the less can it remain satisfied with ethical interpretations of a mysticism which is non-ethical. The need of mysticism which is really intrinsically ethical will make itself felt with ever-increasing force.

From the attempts, so barren of results, to combine knowledge of the Universe and ethics into a single world-view, the thought of mankind must advance to a position where it derives world-view from ethics.

* * *

INDEX

Ādi-Buddha, 121
Advaita, 59, 159
Afghanistan, 20
Agni, 21, 27, 175
Ahiṃsā (not-killing, not harming), viii, 79-87, 101, 102; 229-235
Ahmedabad, 226
Akbar the Great, 208
Americans, 255
Amida-Butsu, 152, 154
Amitābha, Buddha, 121, 125, 140, 144, 148, 152, 164
Ānanda, 94, 95, 114, 121
Anthroposophia, 73
Apocalypse, 162
Aristotle, 5
Arjuna, 182, 184, 190
Aryans, 3, 19, 20, 25, 27, 33, 49, 177, 214
Ārya Samāj, 213, 215
Asceticism, 23, 87, 91, 168, 169, 237
Aśoka, 33, 111, 114, 133
Āśramas, 39
Atharva-Veda, 21, 24, 26
Āthravans, 21
Ātman, 30, 56
Aurobindo Ghose, 249, 254
Avatāras, 175
Avesta, 25, 34
Āyāramgasutta, 81

Bādārāyana, 157
Bentham, Jeremy, 211
Bhagavad-Gītā, 64, 73, 181, 182, 184-199, 203, 220, 222, 245, 251, 258
Bhagavat, 176

Bhakti, 174-184, 216
Bharata, 206
Bhīma, 182
Bible, 173
Bodhi, 89
Bodhidharma, 144, 151
Bodhisattvas, 123, 124, 128
Boer War, 225, 235
Brahmadatta, 107, 108
Brahman, the, 27, 29, 30, 37, 38, 40, 41, 47, 56, 58, 64, 72, 73, 76, 78, 97, 130, 158-166, 175, 197, 210, 242
Brāhmaṇas, 27, 32, 33, 37, 47, 93
Brahmanism, 66, 135-137, 158, 174, 176, 187, 196, 199, 205
Late, 72, 164
Brāhma Samāj, 210-212
Brahmasūtras, 157-159, 163, 164
Brahmins, 25-31, 33, 35-64, 75, 78, 93, 96, 98, 100, 105, 158, 161, 166-172, 174, 176, 178, 211, 214, 242, 244, 250, 251
Bruno, Giordano, 13
Buddha, the, 52, 53, 89-122, 124, 131-133, 136, 144, 145, 149, 152, 154, 155, 181, 186, 193, 203, 238, 251
Buddhism, Ancient Indian, 42, 65, 66, 73, 75, 157, 158, 181, 196, 203
Chinese, 124, 145-7, 149, 150
Japanese, 150-156
Later Indian, 71, 121-137
Mahāyāna, 52, 86, 121-140, 162
Tibetan (Lamaism), 148, 149
Burma, 133, 134
Burnouf, Eugène, 34

Index

Cabral, Francesco, 153
Cambodia, 134
Cāṇḍālas, 26, 171, 172
Caste, 46, 93, 96, 178, 199, 211
Castes, 26
Celibacy, 137, 152, 237
Ceylon, 133, 134, 206
Chên-Tsung, 146
Chicago, World Fair, 219
China, 134, 138-149
Chinese Buddhism. *See* Buddhism
Chinese Thinkers, 1, 34, 84-87, 144-147
Christianity, 12, 216, 218
Chuang-Tse, 140, 141
Chulalongkorn, 134
Civilisation, 240
Colebrooke, Thomas, 34
Compassion, viii, 80-104, 114-116, 119, 123, 125-128, 132, 143. *See also* Ethics
"Confession of Faith," Gandhi's, 235
Confucius, 34, 86, 139, 144-147, 150, 151
Constantinople, Sultan, 226
Copernicus, 215
Cunda, 101

Damayantī, 183
Daśaratha, 205
Dayānand Sarasvatī, 209, 213, 217, 223, 224
Descartes, 62
Deussen, vi, vii, 242
Dhammapada, 112
Dīghāvu, 107, 108
Dīghīti, 107, 108
Docta ignorantia, 263
Dogs, Reincarnation as, 92
Doke, Rev. J. J., 234
Dravidians, 20, 21, 175, 200
Dualism, 10-16, 68, 257
Duperron, Anquetil, 34

Eckhart, Master, 263
Ecstasy, 38, 105, 131, 158
Ethics, general, vi, vii, 8-10, 117, 131, 250, 251, 259-265
 among the Brahmins, 53, 54, 63, 72, 105, 118, 242
 Christian, 154
 in Chinese Thought and Chinese Buddhism, 84-87
 in Hinduism, 180, 199, 200, 205
 in Jainism, 77, 78, 84, 105
 in Japanese Buddhism, 154
 in Mahāyāna Buddhism, 131, 133
 in Manu's Law Book, 166-173
 in the Bhagavad-Gītā, 222
 in the Kural, 200-205
 in the Sāṃkhya doctrine, 72, 105
 of the Buddha, 99-113, 117, 120, 137, 154, 180
 of R. Tagore, 243

Fah-Hien, 138
Fasting, 89, 92
Fichte, 13, 192, 240, 245, 247, 248, 253, 258
Fouillée, Alfred, 247
Fu-Yi, 146

Gandhi, Mahatma, 137, 225-238
Genghiz Khan, 147
Genkū, 152
Gentz, Friedrich von, 190
Ghose. *See* Aurobindo
Gnostics and Gnosticism, 4, 44, 52, 68
God, 184-195, 207, 212, 213, 217, 222, 239, 242, 244-246, 248
Gosāla (Makkhali), 88
Go-Toba, 152
Gratitude, 112
Graul, Karl, 202
Gunas, 69, 70, 73
Guyau, Jean Marie, 247

Index

Hackmann, H., 142
Hamilton, Alexander, 34
Hand-spinning and weaving, 227, 228
Hanumat, 206
Han-Yü, 146
Hastings, Warren, 34
Hastings' *Encyclopaedia of Religion and Ethics*, 212
Hegel, 13, 68, 253
Hemacandra, 82
Hīnayāna, 122
Hindi language, 207
Hinduism, 58, 120, 134-137, 163, 174-184, 193-200, 205, 210, 218, 223
Hsin-Tsung, 144
Hsüan-Tsang, 138
Hsüan-Tsung, 146
Hui-Tsung, 146
Humboldt, W. von, 190

Indra, 20, 175
International Buddhist Society, 156
Islam, 137, 196, 208, 216

Jainism, 42, 65, 66, 73, 75-88, 91, 99, 100-105, 135, 137, 157, 158
Janaka, 23
Japan, 134, 150
Japanese Buddhism. *See* Buddhism
Jātakas, 104
Java, 137
Jesuits, 153
Jesus, 4-6, 113, 116, 117, 162, 209, 216, 234
Jīvaka, 101
Jōdo sect, 151, 154
Jōdo-Shinshū sect, 152-154
Jones, William, 34

Kabīr, 208
Kālī, 175, 216, 217

Kan-Ying-P'ien, 84-87, 143
Kant, 12, 188, 240, 264
Karman, 70, 78, 98, 99
Karmayoga, 221
Kāryamoha, 132
Keshab Chandra Sen, 209, 212, 213, 216, 217, 223, 224
King, the, in Manu's Law Book, 168-170
Kōbō, 150
Korea, 134, 150
Krishṇa, 73, 174, 182, 184-186, 188-190, 205
Kṣatriyas, 26
Kublai-Khan, 147, 149
Kumārapāla, 82
Kural, 200-205
Kurus, 181, 182

Lalitavistara, 124
Lamas, 148, 149
Lao-Tse, 139, 141, 144-146
Leibnitz, 69
Lhassa, 148, 149
Lieh-Tse, 140
Līlā, 246
Love, Active, 109, 113, 193, 199. *See also* Ethics
Luther, 91, 92, 152, 153

Mahābhārata, 73, 181, 182, 205, 212
Mahāvīra, 79
Mahendra, 133
Maitreyī, 37, 130
Makkhali. *See* Gosāla
Manes, 40
Manichæism, 146
Manu's Law Book, 166-173, 184, 201, 212
Marriage, 136, 137, 200, 201, 214, 236, 237
Māyā, 59, 60, 72, 131, 158, 159, 165, 185
Meat-eating, 101, 102, 203
Meng-Tse (Mencius), 34, 86

Mesa, 33
Metempsychosis. *See* Reincarnation
Milinda, 90, 98
Milindapañha, 90, 98
Ming-Ti, Emperor, 138, 139
Mitra, 27, 175
Mi-Tse, 86
Mohammed Dara Shakoh, 34
Mohammedanism, 137, 218, 226, 227
Mokṣa, 237
Monasticism, 87, 93, 94, 104, 105, 107, 109, 110, 114, 141, 142, 146, 178, 179
Mongolia, 148, 149
Monism, 10-15, 159
Monotheism, 28, 58, 163, 176, 223
Moon-myth, 48, 49
Myōan Eisai, 151
Mysticism, in general, vi, 11, 28, 77, 194, 250, 256-258, 262-265
  in the Bhagavad-Gītā, 190
  Brahmanic, 42, 43, 53-56, 61, 65, 70, 72, 73, 76, 134, 163, 164, 177, 194, 197, 198, 210, 224
  Christian, 177, 178
  Greco-oriental, 68
  Hindu (Bhakti), 134, 164, 174-184, 197, 198
  of Identity, 47, 60, 66, 67, 262
  supra-ethical, 54, 60
  Western, 190

Nāgārjuna, 125, 132
Nāgasena, 90, 98
Nala, 182
Nāmdev, 198
Nānak, 208
Neoplatonism, 4, 13
Nepal, 134
Neumann, 105
New Testament, 225
Nichiren, 154, 155

Nietzsche, 36, 44, 173, 253
Nirvāṇa, 97, 99, 100, 115, 122, 124, 128
Nobunaga, 155
Nuns, 94, 95

Om, 38
Oupnek'hat, 34

Pāli, 90, 124
Pāṇḍu (Pāṇḍava), 182
Panjāb, 20
Pantheism, 13, 154
Parātmasamatā, 129
Pariahs, 26, 207
Pārśvanātha, 79
Passive resistance, 231-234
Paul, Saint, 94, 102, 107, 128, 162, 186
Perfection, Doctrine of, 113, 117, 118
Pessimism, 247
Polyandry, 182
Polytheism, 174, 233
Portuguese, 208
Prākrit, 34
Prakṛti, 68
Priests, 23, 147, 173
Prophets, Jewish, 11
Purāṇas, 181
Puruṣa, 68

Quietism, 178

Radhakrishṇan, S., 249
Rajayoga, 221
Rām Mohan Ray, 209-211, 223, 224
Rāma, 175, 205-208
Rāmakrishna, vi, 209, 216-221, 223, 224
Rāmānanda, 207, 208
Rāmānuja, 197, 198, 207, 210
Rāmāyana, 181, 205
Rāvana, 206
Redemption, Doctrine of, in

Index

Brahmanic Mysticism, 95, 136, 177
  the Buddha's doctrine of, 115, 121, 136
  in Gandhi's teaching, 237
  in Japan, 153
  in Late Buddhism, 163-165
  in Mahāyāna Buddhism, 127
Reincarnation, 42, 47-51, 53-56, 61, 62, 65, 71, 72, 75-78, 88, 124, 222, 223
  the Buddha's teaching of, 97, 99, 106, 161, 163
Renaissance, 5, 57
Rig-Veda, 21, 26, 30, 38, 47, 175
Roman Emperors, 164
Ruskin, 228
Ryōbu-Shintō, 150

Sacrifice, Animal, 44, 82
Sacrificial word and rites, 24
Saddharmapundarīka, 124
Sādhanā, 238-241, 245-247
Sākhyas, 89, 125
Sāma-Veda, 21
Śamkara, 56, 57, 73, 159, 160, 162-165, 177, 197
Samkhāras, 97
Sāmkhya doctrine, 65-76, 78, 79, 91, 99, 105, 121, 135, 157, 158, 161
Sāmkhyakārikā, 67, 73
Samsāra. See Reincarnation
Sannyāsin, 239
Sanskrit, 20, 34, 90, 124
Śāntideva, 125
Śāntiniketan, 238
Sāriputta, 100, 109
Satyavant, 183
Sāvitrī, 183
Schelling, 13, 253
Schlegel, Friedrich W., 34, 190
Scholasticism, Brahmanic, 158, 159, 196, 197
Schopenhauer, vi, vii, 34, 242
Semitism, 173

Shaftesbury, 240, 247, 248
Shamans, 22, 23
Shinran, 152, 154
Shinto religion, 150, 151, 155, 156
Siam, 133, 134
Silk-worms, 103
Sītā, 206
Śiva, 30, 175, 205, 220
Slavery, 94
Solomon, Song of, 177, 201, 246
Soma drink, 22
Soul in all things. See Universal Soul
Spinoza, 13
Spirit of the Universe, 134
Srong-btsan-sgam-po, King, 147
Stage-play, the World as a, 2, 245, 253, 258
Steiner, Rudolph, 73, 74
Stoicism, 5
Şuan, King, 86
Śūdras, 26, 93
Sukhāvatī, 122, 125
Sukhāvatīryūha, 125
Sumatra, 137
Śūnyatā, 132
Suttapiṭaka, 112
Sūtra with 42 Sections, 139
Sūtras, 157, 197
Svāmin. See Vivekānanda

Tagore, Debendranāth, 209, 211-214, 217, 223, 224
Tagore, Rabīndranāth, 197, 209, 238-249, 258
Taoism, 139-146
Tao-Te-King, 140, 144
Tat twam asi, 35, 43, 48, 262
Tea, 151
Technical expressions, ix
Tibet, 134, 147-149, 182
Tiruvaḷḷuvar, 200
Tripitaka, 90, 134
Truth, Twofold, 163
Truthfulness, 45, 46, 87
Tsungs, 144

Tsung-kha-pa, 148
Tukārām, 198
Tulsī-Dās, 208
Turkestan, 138
Turtle, 115

Universal Soul, 32, 49, 50, 52-57, 59-62, 65, 72, 76, 80, 93, 95, 97, 99, 105, 157, 160, 161, 197, 248
Untouchables, 227, 229
Upanishads, 3, 25, 26, 32-67, 73, 76-78, 81, 87, 97, 130, 157, 158, 160, 210, 212, 224, 225, 242, 243, 248, 262

Vaiśyas, 26, 225
Vālmīki, 205
Varuna, 27, 175
Vedas, v, 19, 21, 29, 33, 136, 157, 172-175, 181, 207, 215, 220, 225, 241
Vedānta, 157, 197, 216, 220
Vishnu, 30, 175, 197, 198, 205-207
Vivekānanda, Svāmin, vi, 209, 218-221, 223, 224, 254, 255
Völkerwanderung, 142

Way, the Eightfold, 109
Widow-burning, 171, 211

Wilkins, Charles, 34, 190
Will-to-live, 103, 263
Woman, in Manu's Laws, 171
  an inferior being, 95
  can attain a state of bliss, 152
World and life affirmation, vii, 1-10, 47, 56, 92, 119, 120, 136, 153, 156, 179, 181, 196, 201, 224, 238, 239, 242, 246, 250-258, 264
  and life negation, vii, viii, 1-10, 56, 64, 76-78, 87, 92, 100, 103, 108, 113, 116-120, 136, 137, 153, 156, 179, 180, 181, 196, 199, 201, 224, 238, 239, 242, 246, 250, 256
  periods, 71, 121, 161
  renunciation of the, 91, 92, 181
Wu-Tsung, 146

Xavier, Francis, 155

Yājñavalkya, 23, 37, 41, 56, 130
Yajur-Veda, 21
Yao-Ch'ung, 146
Yogins (Yoga), 22, 31, 37, 38, 63, 70

Zarathustra, 1, 11, 21, 28, 146, 176, 208
Zen sect, 151, 154

OTHER BEACON PAPERBACKS IN PHILOSOPHY

BP9   Buber, Martin — BETWEEN MAN AND MAN

BP64 Buber, Martin — PATHS IN UTOPIA

BP7   Cassirer, Ernst — THE PHILOSOPHY OF THE ENLIGHTENMENT

BP48 Dewey, John — RECONSTRUCTION IN PHILOSOPHY

BP74 Frankel, Charles — THE CASE FOR MODERN MAN

BP35 Gandhi, Mohandas K. — AN AUTOBIOGRAPHY: The Story of My Experiments with Truth

BP50 Gierke, Otto — NATURAL LAW AND THE THEORY OF SOCIETY, 1500-1800

BP60 Grube, G. M. A. — PLATO'S THOUGHT

BP17 Halévy, Elie — THE GROWTH OF PHILOSOPHIC RADICALISM

BP91 Heine, Heinrich — RELIGION AND PHILOSOPHY IN GERMANY

BP15 Huizinga, Johan — HOMO LUDENS: A Study of the Play Element in Culture

BP1   Schweitzer, Albert — ALBERT SCHWEITZER: An Anthology

BP70 Schweitzer, Albert — THE ANIMAL WORLD OF ALBERT SCHWEITZER

BP11 Weil, Simone — THE NEED FOR ROOTS

BP72 Whitehead, Alfred North — THE FUNCTION OF REASON

35-202